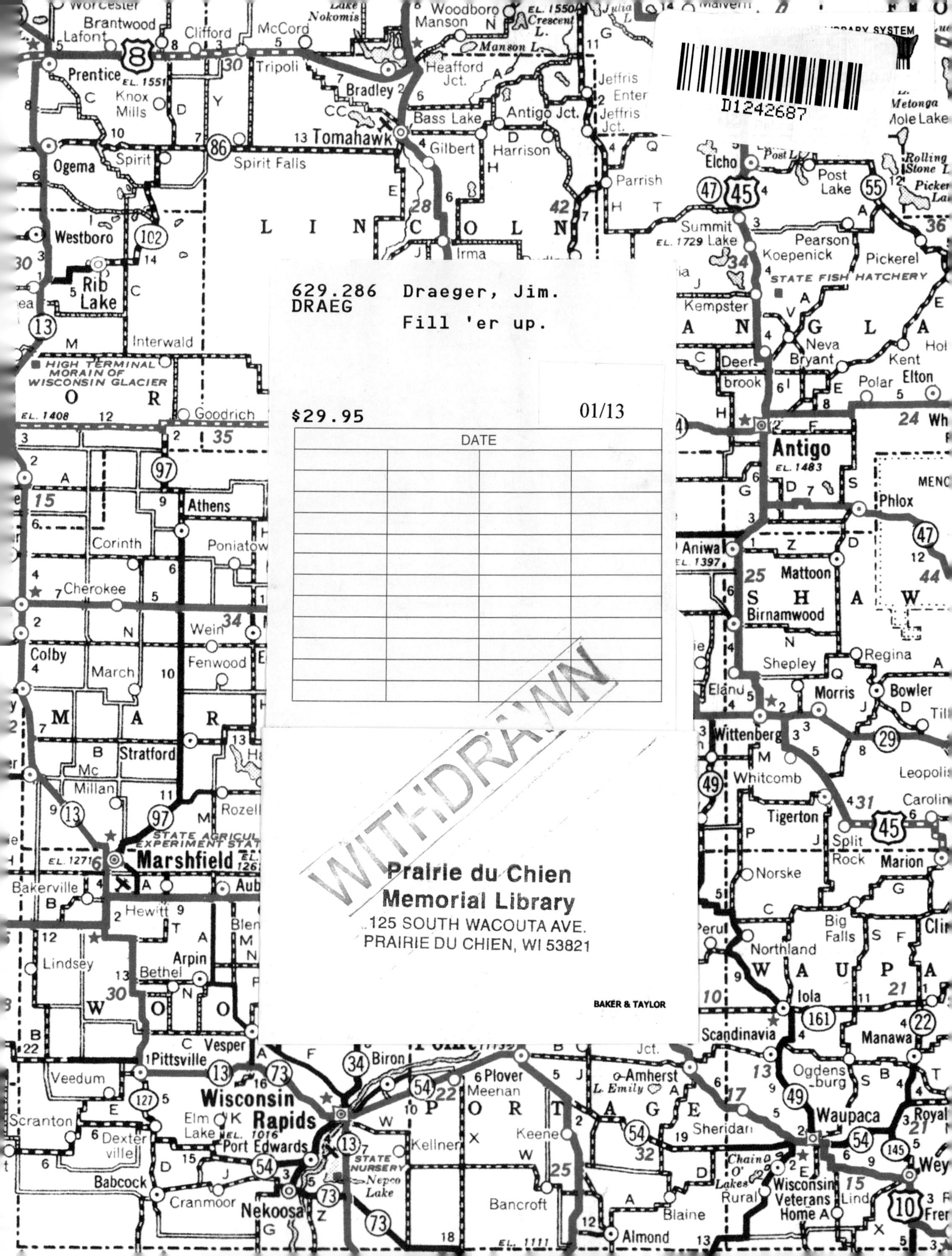

D1242687
629.286 DRAEG
Draeger, Jim.
Fill 'er up.
$29.95
01/13
DATE
WITHDRAWN
Prairie du Chien Memorial Library
125 SOUTH WACOUTA AVE.
PRAIRIE DU CHIEN, WI 53821
BAKER & TAYLOR

Fill 'er Up

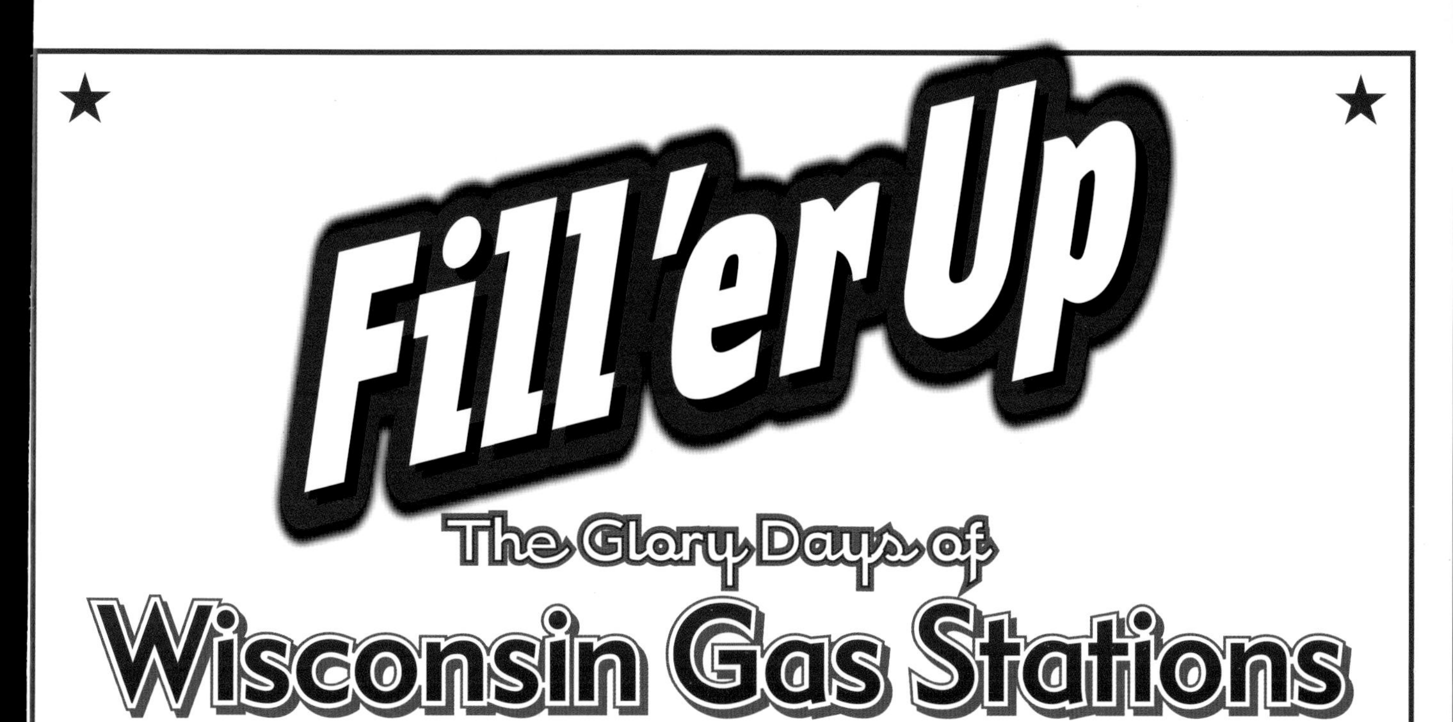

Fill'er Up

The Glory Days of Wisconsin Gas Stations

Jim Draeger
Mark Speltz

Wisconsin Historical Society Press

Places along the Way

Published by the Wisconsin Historical Society Press
Publishers since 1855

Publication of this book was made possible, in part, by funding from the Wisconsin Department of Transportation, the John C. Geilfuss Fellowship, and the D. C. Everest Fellowship.

www.wisconsinhistory.org

Photographs identified with PH, WHi, or WHS are from the Society's collections; address inquiries about such photos to the Visual Materials Archivist at Wisconsin Historical Society, 816 State Street, Madison, WI 53706.

Printed in Wisconsin, U.S.A.
Designed by Brad Norr Design
12 11 10 09 08   1 2 3 4 5

Library of Congress Cataloging-in-Publication Data

Draeger, Jim.
Fill 'er up : the glory days of Wisconsin gas stations / Jim Draeger, Mark Speltz.
p. cm.
Includes bibliographical references and index.
ISBN 978-0-87020-393-0 (hardcover : alk. paper) 1. Service stations—Wisconsin—History—20th century. 2. Historic buildings—Wisconsin—History—20th century. 3. Architecture, Industrial—Wisconsin—History—20th century. 4. Automobile travel—United States—History—20th century. I. Speltz, Mark. II. Title. III. Title: Fill her up.
TL153.D73 2009
629.28'609775—dc22
2008023236

Front cover: Independence station, WHS Accession 2008/088, photo by Mark Fay. Back cover: cottage-style station (top), Courtesy of O. J. Thompto; Monroe station (middle), WHS Accession 2008/088, photo by Mark Fay; Wadhams pagoda-style station (bottom), Courtesy of Jim Draeger. Spine: WHS Accession 2008/088, photo by Mark Fay. Front flap: WHi Image ID 34477.

Page iii: Courtesy of O. J. Thompto; page vi: first row (l to r) WHi Image ID 16691, WHi Image ID 35804, PH 6058 2575-C-2; second row (l to r) Courtesy of UWM Libraries, Archives Department, UWM Mss 131, Box 10, F 3 #87329-x, WHi Image ID 40423, Courtesy of O. J. Thompto; third row (l to r): WHi Image ID 54922, WHi Image ID 24513, WHi Image ID 58456, Courtesy of Wayne Hillary; fourth row (l to r): WHi Image ID 57116, Courtesy of O. J. Thompto, WHi Image ID 34477; page v: WHi Image ID 58455; pages 58, 86, 144, and 168: WHi Image ID 58457; pages 59 and 87: Courtesy of Marjorie Clark Takton, photos by Joel Heiman; pages 145 and 169: Northwoods Petroleum Museum, photos by Joel Heiman.

∞ The paper used in this publication meets the minimum requirements of the American National Standard for Information Sciences—Permanence of Paper for Printed Library Materials, ANSI Z39.48-1992.

We lovingly dedicate this book to our spouses, Kari Speltz and Cindy Draeger, and Jim's son, Nick Draeger. We recognize their sacrifices and help throughout the many months that we immersed ourselves in the world of grease and gas. Their enthusiasm and love made our work a pleasure and the trip a fun adventure. Their full-service support kept our jalopies on the road as we rattled and clattered our way to completion.

VALVOLINE
VALVOLINE GASOLINE
SUPREME
STANDARD RED CROWN
GRAND OPENING
FRI. 8th. - SAT. 9th.
BUBBLE GUM
KIDDIES
STANDARD OIL PRODUCTS
PURE
REGULAR
TIRES
ATLAS
TEXACO
We fix
Farmers Union
CO OP
MAY 56
97-105

Contents

Preface

As we look out onto the built landscape of Wisconsin, it is our unmistakable conclusion that gas stations are among the most ephemeral of all buildings. Where hundreds of single-purpose gas stations defined by familiar and personal service once stood in Wisconsin's largest cities and dotted its highways and busy corners, only handfuls remain. Today we fill up anonymously at convenience stores, often paying at the pump with no human interaction. Stations have fallen victim to competition, obsolescence, changing transportation needs and housing patterns, as well as stronger environmental regulations. Historic stations are becoming a rarity; those that remain are artifacts of the twentieth century's struggle to accommodate the revolutionary changes brought by the automobile. It is our interest in capturing the stories connected with these fleeting remnants that has led us to write this book.

Gas stations celebrate the history of our automotive culture. We have found strong popular interest in the topic, which we believe is because these stations are part of the personal stories of so many people. Gas stations are indispensable background buildings in the daily lives of most of us. In a culture shaped by the automobile, stations are an unavoidable necessity. People may not dwell upon the evolution of gas stations or their historical importance, but they have directly experienced those stations. Their lives have intersected with the architecture of gas stations and been influenced and shaped by their presence. The ubiquity of gas stations has meant that the memories of many people are intertwined with stations, whether their family members were owners or operators, they got their first job pumping gas, or they hung out at a local station as kids.

Architecture, no matter how humble and seemingly insignificant, is a reflection of who we are and what we value. Buildings are the physical embodiment of the personal stories of those who built them. More important, those individual stories form the warp and weft of our collective history. They are shaped by broader historical patterns, formed by the social, cultural, economic, political, and technological forces of the time that created them. In this manner, buildings are touchstones to the past, three-dimensional storybooks that allow us to immerse ourselves in an earlier time and hear the echo of those who have come before us.

Our interest in the stories of gas stations stems from our conviction that stations are the most potent symbols of the automobile's role in transforming twentieth-century American culture. They are the pivotal historical artifacts of the auto age, analogous to the late-nineteenth-century railroad depot. Just as the past decades have seen railroad depots rediscovered, restored, and rehabilitated for new uses by those who wish to keep the memory of railroading alive, we believe that gas stations will become prized community assets. Readers will discover that interest has already awakened in preserving historic gas stations. Time will see communities embrace these buildings and value them.

As ubiquitous as gas stations are to our modern society, they are possibly the most ephemeral of all commercial buildings. Built for a specialized use in a highly competitive business, the majority of all gas stations ever constructed in Wisconsin have already been demolished. Many had a useful life of no more than a decade before their owners replaced them with a new station, remodeled them to keep up with marketplace trends, abandoned them, or adapted them to a new use. All but the most modern gas stations included in this book are rare survivors, and even those face only a slim chance of surviving until the public sees them as something worthy of preservation. As we prepared the book for publication, a chance trip past Harry Klippel's station just south of Hazelhurst found it to be demolished, underscoring the fragility of all of the stations listed in this book. If you plan to visit any of the stations depicted in these pages, keep in mind that not every one will still be standing.

Preservation of remaining stations cannot come too soon. It is our hope that our celebration of these stations will spur interest in saving this chapter in American history and readers will recognize that gas stations are about more than just gas: they are touchstones to understanding how the auto shaped the twentieth century. Although we focus on Wisconsin in this book, the story is national in scope. Each gas station's story connects it to a larger tale that is written many times in communities across the country.

Acknowledgments

Thanks to Michael Stevens, Wisconsin's state historic preservation officer, for his support and encouragement, and Kathy Borkowski, director of the Wisconsin Historical Society Press, for her faith in us to deliver a manuscript—and her gentle prodding when we fell behind. Many other staff at the Wisconsin Historical Society gave us tips on stations, shared information, helped with research, listened patiently to endless gas station stories, and helped out whenever asked, most notably historian Joe DeRose and architectural historian Daina Penkiunas. Our thanks to David Hestad and Carol Larson of Wisconsin Public Television, who had faith in our boast that the history of the twentieth century could be told in the gas station and supported us with a companion documentary of the same title. They shared contacts, information, interviews, research, and photos and made an enormous, largely unseen, contribution to this book. We'd also like to thank our editors, Stephen Schenkenberg, Melissa Johnson, and Laura Kearney, who are responsible for honing, polishing, and giving form to our manuscript.

We are grateful to Marjorie Clark Takton, daughter of Emory T. Clark of Clark Oil Company, and the many other descendants of the original station owners who shared stories, family photographs, and much more. Our thanks, too, to the various researchers who dug through old newspapers in search of articles about grand openings, advertisements, and other leads that helped bring these stations to life: Rose Edmunds, Sam Finesurrey, Camilla Hansen, Mallory Kirby, and Alison Reveille. And thanks to John Nondorf of the Wisconsin Historical Society Press for his expertise in researching and preparing the images herein for publication.

We are grateful for the time and assistance received along the way from both past and present station owners, family members, and those who help maintain their community's local history. We extend our thanks to many people, but especially the following: Dick Ambrose, Ken and Julie Arbuckle, Ervin and Marilyn Bankes, Charlie and Pat Berg, Robert Broetzman, Wally and Sandy Copeland, Priscilla Dorn Cutler, Marian Engfer, Matt Figi, Bob Hedgecock, Gary and Judy Heise, Norman Hoeft, William Jannke, Barbara Koehler, the Kohlmeier family, Marisa Kosobucki, Joe Krupp, Cliff Leppke, Dennis McCann, Gloria

Morgan, Loren and Rose Nelson, Daniel O'Keefe, Bob and Patrice Olin, Marilyn Owens, Todd Owens, Kitty Rankin, Elaine Reisner, Ray Savera, Monty Schiro, Keith Sculle, Tom Shambeau, William Siebel II, Jim and Phyllis Spangler, Corinne Tetzlaff, Kay Walters, Pam Weinhammer, Dee Wells, Dan and Duane Wiegand, Nola Wieland, Gail Winnie, and Warren Witwen.

A special thanks to O. J. Thompto, petroliana collector extraordinaire, who has been tracking down ephemera and documentation on gas stations for many decades and unselfishly opened his personal collection to us. Warren Baley, current president of Steel King, and his office manager Chris Jacobs opened the Steel King company files to us and were accommodating to our every request. We are grateful for their welcome assistance. And thanks to Ed Jacobson, owner of the Northwoods Petroleum Museum in Three Lakes, who now shares his interest in the gas industry with those who visit his collection in the North Woods. Joel Heiman of the Wisconsin Historical Society Press captured the character of the place in the images of Ed's memorabilia found in the following pages.

The photography of Mark Fay contributes greatly to the appeal of this book. It is challenging to convey a sense of historical import to such lowly and often-neglected buildings. Mark's sumptuous photographs help to evoke the beauty of simple utility. In addition to being a skillful architectural photographer, Mark has been a great friend, and we are greatly in his debt.

Fill 'er Up

Smiling Sinclair attendants in Waukesha, 1938. WHi Image ID 2090

Wisconsin Gas Stations

Tracing Their Evolution

Economist John Kenneth Galbraith called gas stations "the most repellent piece of architecture of the last two thousand years. There are far more of them than are needed. Usually they are filthy. Their merchandise is hideously packaged and garishly displayed.... Stations should be excluded entirely from most streets and highways."[1] Although reviled by Galbraith and many others, it is impossible to imagine the auto age without gas stations. The stories of gas stations are woven into the fabric of modern culture.

Gas stations have an unusual place in the built environment. For auto owners, gas stations are a basic necessity, fueling a lifestyle made possible by and built around the car. For much of the twentieth century, our experience with auto fueling was personal, built on a familiar relationship with our neighborhood station and its full-service attendants. Stations were a social node, an accidental meeting place, where the attendants moderated our interactions, dispensing not only gasoline but travel reports, neighborhood news, and other tidbits that connected their customers to the larger world.

As inevitable and essential as gas stations might seem today, irresistible historical forces shaped their development. As gas stations have helped to shape the modern world, so has the world shaped them.

In 1926, this Pennsylvania Oil Company service station in Madison was voted the country's second-most beautiful gas station. Its storybook design might have made Galbraith think twice. WHi Image ID 6357

Begin the Beguine
Early Days of the Auto Age

Automotive historians generally credit German inventors Gottlieb Daimler and Karl Benz with developing the

Wisconsin inventor Thomas Jeffery (his company later merged with Nash Motors) in an early car, 1897. WHi Image ID 40834

first successful and practical gasoline-powered vehicles in the mid-1880s and ushering in the age of modern automobiles. By 1905, there were fifty thousand cars in the United States. The automobile was a strange, belching, sputtering beast and an odd metal intrusion in a primarily agrarian world. The public response was a mixture of curiosity and bemusement, as indicated by this account, published in the *Milwaukee Telegram,* of the first auto parade in Milwaukee in 1900:

> Seven strange looking vehicles burst into fits of coughing, shook with asthmatic convulsions and rattled and creaked down Grand av. The crowd that stood about roared with laughter. People held their sides as they watched the drivers being bounced up and down on the seats of their bucking-bronco chariots. All the way from Thirty-fifth st. and Grand av. to the lake the contraptions hacked and coughed, belched forth clouds of vapor, dripped oil and grease and emitted weird noises that rang through the air for blocks around.[2]

Within two decades, the United States had six million cars, and this new form of transportation had moved from oddity to necessity—a transformation with profound cultural impacts. As the number of autos grew, a period of rapid experimentation and innovation ensued as cities and countryside evolved to accommodate this new transportation form. The auto heightened the importance of good streets and roads, city planning became more systematic and regulated, and government tightened ordinances and zoning laws. The physical layout of cities changed, and the places where people lived, worked, learned, shopped, and visited changed as well, ushering in new lifestyles that differed markedly from those of the pre-auto age.

The First Automobile Licenses in Wisconsin

Although the laws of Wisconsin had required that automobile drivers yield to horses since the car's first appearance in the state, Wisconsin did not require drivers to register their vehicles until 1905. The first car registrations cost one dollar and were elaborate affairs. According to the Waterloo Courier, the documents were gold-sealed, seven inches square, and could "pass as a marriage certificate."[1] At the time, there was no "driver's license," just the auto registration, and no required exam; the first written and practical test for all drivers was instituted by New Jersey in 1913.[2] While Wisconsin motorists had to carry a driver's license that indicated their fitness to drive beginning in 1928, they did not face a mandatory exam and road test until 1941.[3]

Notes

1. "He Had the First Auto License; Always First Wheels in Town," *Waterloo Courier*, January 29, 1925.
2. "New York's Auto Exports Increase—Big Jump in Cars Shipped Last Year—New Jersey Examines All Drivers," *New York Times*, July 14, 1913.
3. WI Statutes 85.08 (1929); Laws of WI, Chapter 206 (1941).

Lugging Jugs and Curbside Pumps

Gas Retailing at the Dawn of the Auto Age

In the nineteenth century, gasoline was an unwanted byproduct of kerosene production, and processors typically discarded it, until scientists discovered that its ability to vaporize at low temperatures made it an ideal fuel source. Gottlieb Daimler's invention of a prototypical gasoline-fueled engine in 1885 effectively ushered in the auto age. The development of the internal combustion engine created the need for a means to distribute gasoline, giving rise to a rudimentary network of bulk stations that warehoused gas aboveground.

Madison's first bulk station was built on a site purchased in the fall of 1900 by Theodore M. Leonard and his partner Mr. Ellis for the Standard Oil Company, which at that time had a monopoly on gasoline refining and distribution.[3] Far from today's network of convenient and accessible refueling, Leonard and Ellis' bulk oil depot dispensed unfiltered gas into autos from either metal or glass storage containers. For the automotive pioneer clad in a long frock coat, dust cap, and driving goggles, maneuvering an awkward container over the inconveniently placed fuel tank of his or her car, while simultaneously juggling a funnel and a chamois cloth filter, was an

Hastily erected sheds housed the first gas stations.
Courtesy of O. J. Thompto

adventure requiring strength and dexterity. Clearly, the smelly, dirty, and dangerous work of refueling an automobile required much improvement before automobiles could become a mainstay of transportation.

The introduction of filtered gasoline by 1904 allowed broader distribution of fuel. A cleaner, more reliable grade of fuel led to the expansion of gas retailing via a slapdash network of existing blacksmith shops, general stores, bicycle shops, and machine shops. Motorists continued to dispense gasoline by jug or can, and although gas became more available, the distribution system was still immature. The absence of a reliable roadside network for dispensing gasoline is clear from a September 13, 1904, *Wisconsin State Journal* article that notes: "Philip Denu returned last week from the western part of the state, where he purchased a team of fine horses. These he will use for delivering oils and gasoline to the various part of the city."[4] Ironically, Denu's horse team delivered gasoline door-to-door to fuel the early autos that in the next several decades would end the horse-and-buggy age.

In 1907, American scientist Charles Palmer developed a patented process to "crack" crude oil, subjecting it to high pressure and temperature to force the distillation of gasoline. His improved method revolutionized the industry, increasing the yield of gasoline from crude oil, improving its purity, and paving the way for modern transportation. Oddly enough, as the auto age progressed, Palmer never owned a car or learned to drive.

Before the development of gas stations, storing volatile fuel in containers in a haphazard collection of existing buildings increased the risk of fire or explosion. One solution was to build diminutive, single-purpose storage buildings a safe distance from other buildings. About 1907, A. M. Hansen of Waupaca built a tiny outhouse-sized brick shed to dispense gas. He located the building midblock on Jefferson Street, equidistant between Hansen's Machinery Hall and his auto service. His practical and economic solution isolated the

The tiny brick building in the center is A. M. Hansen's Waupaca gas shed. He stored gasoline a safe distance from his other buildings. Courtesy of Wahlen J. Doran

aboveground storage of gasoline and minimized the threat to neighboring buildings. Within a few years, early freestanding gasoline storage buildings such as Hansen's became full-fledged gas stations.

The dangers of storing volatile fuel in containers forced more innovations. Within a few years, underground storage and the gas pump's hose-and-nozzle system allowed an operator to dispense gasoline directly into the fuel tank. Reliable and safe handling of gasoline transformed the chaotic collection of fueling depots into a modern service industry. The introduction of gas pumps led directly to the development of ancillary "stations" to house the attendants, and the gas station was born.

It's a Gas, Gas, Gas

The First Stations

Early innovators hastily and cheaply erected the first gas stations. These utilitarian sheds suited the rapidly evolving automotive transportation system and served as experimental prototypes for the development of more standardized station types. Stations needed to provide little more than shelter for attendants, minimal business space, and limited storage for the ancillary products associated with gas retailing. Retailers did not give much thought to the aesthetics or efficiency of station designs, and many stations were little more than rudimentary shacks. As a roadside building, the gas station had no real precursors; consequently, there were no consumer expectations of what gas stations should look like or how they would function. The community horse trough was probably the closest pre-auto corollary to the functional requirements of dispensing fuel.

Uncle Al's Fill Station in Kilbourn (today Wisconsin Dells) served up gas as well as boat tickets. WHi Image ID 57117

The ubiquitous "stand-alone" gas station was not the only means of dispensing this fuel. The gasoline-distribution system evolved from the pre-existing kerosene trade, so businesses such as general stores and hardware stores added gasoline to their product line. In the 1910s and 1920s, motorists bought gas from livery stables, dry goods stores, grocery stores, and blacksmith shops that sold it as a sideline to their normal trade.

As the volume of sales increased, the early system of dispensing gasoline by hand could no longer keep up, so these businesses installed underground tanks and gas pumps. Because gas retailing was an add-on to existing businesses, these were not true gas stations. Nineteenth-century commercial buildings, which were often built up to the sidewalk and filled the lot line, were poorly suited to selling gas. Owners who lacked sufficient space set their pumps on the edge of the road, on the sidewalk, or in the public right-of-way. Curbside pumps quickly became a commonplace sight in both city and countryside. City planners noted the congestion caused by lines of autos backing up on the road and the dangers of errant drivers dislodging curbside pumps. In "Curbing the Curb Pump," an article in the August 1923 issue of *American City* magazine, C. A. Crosser exclaimed, "Many American cities are making a vigorous fight for the freedom of their streets."[5] Safety concerns led to changes in ordinances and building codes that eliminated haphazard arrangements. By the mid-1920s, many places banned curbside pumps, increasing the popularity of the stand-alone station.

The Droster Store in the town of Burke sold groceries and gasoline. WHi Image ID 31934

Curbside pumps like these in Norwalk were a common fixture of city streets in the early part of the twentieth century. WHi Image ID 57113

Although major oil companies such as Standard Oil and Shell Oil quickly established retail operations, most stations were small "mom-and-pop" businesses, entrepreneurial start-ups that took varied forms. Cornelius Trapp took advantage of his home's location along a highway passing through Hartland (see page 98). He graded the northern part of the lot and wrapped a gas station around a portion of the front and north side elevation of his residence. Other owners, such as the Kochenderfer family of Cochrane (see page 60), created living spaces on the second floor, above the station office, a testament to the long hours of owner/operator stations.

Paving the Way

Early Roads

Economy was a paramount consideration for many station owners. Frugal investment in the physical infrastructure allowed more rapid expansion for those who owned multiple locations and minimized the risk of an unprofitable location. As planners plotted out highways and arterial routes through cities, yesterday's main route might become today's backwater, leaving

Visible Pumps

An inherent problem with early fueling was a lack of consumer confidence. When drivers had used a bucket, hose, or funnel to fuel up, they could perceive how much and what quality gasoline they were getting. With blind pumps, they feared cheating owners could sell impure gas or rig the pumps to give unfair measure. Even with no ill will on the part of the operator, the hand-cranking mechanism and dial indicator were notoriously inaccurate.

Pump manufacturers provided a solution to this problem: visible pumps that routed gasoline through a glass chamber atop the pumps, complete with gallon-mark lines, so the customer could watch the fuel as it was dispensed. Inventor John Tokheim created the first of these by 1906, and Bowser, Wayne, and other manufacturers soon copied this innovation.[1]

Ironically, the visible pump was not as good as it looked. Dishonest retailers could still cheat by moving the gallon marks, and, because of the natural heat expansion of the glass and fuel, the machines gave less fuel for the dollar on hot days. Later pumps still featured a small glass bubble with a spinner inside to show the movement of fuel, while a bell chimed out the gallons even after the true visible pump had become obsolete.

Courtesy of O. J. Thompto

Notes

1. Michael Witzel, *Gas Stations Coast to Coast* (Osceola, WI: MBI Publishing, 2000), p. 44.

a once-successful gas station stranded off the beaten path.

Frustrated by traffic lost to Highway 15 (later U.S. Highway 41) several blocks away, Cudahy station owner Harry Baumgarten, as reported in the *Watertown Daily News*, "performed the miracle of re-locating [*sic*] a highway over night." Baumgarten repainted three miles of highway signs, directing traffic to his station. A traveler became suspicious when detour signs ended at Baumgarten's station and notified the local sheriff, who advised Baumgarten to "get busy with his paint brush" and restore the signage.[6]

Early rural roads often were nearly impassable for automobiles.
WHi Image ID 40308

Early highways were nothing more than routes strung out along existing rural roads and urban streets. Conditions were poor at best, and in many cases roads were impassable, owing in part to a clause in the Wisconsin state constitution prohibiting state funding for transportation projects. Conceived as a safeguard to keep tax dollars from supporting private interests, the

Gas of Many Hues

From the dawn of the automobile to the present, colored gasoline has always had a practical purpose. Various colors have been used to alert consumers to leaded gas, to denote aviation fuel or high-performance racing fuel, and to keep commercial truck drivers from using untaxed diesel intended for farm equipment.

With the advent of visible pumps in the 1910s, however, dyed gas quickly became part of marketing campaigns. Initially, the color distinguished the fuel's grade: regular gas came in amber tones, while premium was a regal blue, red, or purple, and clear fuel fed farmers' tractors. Soon, major retailers were using color to brand their gasoline. Texaco chose green, Esso was red, and Sunoco flowed in pretty blue.

Clockface pumps, which were invented in 1923 and made hand cranking obsolete thanks to a motor-driven pump mechanism, soon replaced the slow and outmoded visible pumps. Multicolored gasoline disappeared soon thereafter.[1]

Notes

1. Michael Witzel, *Gas Stations Coast to Coast* (Osceola, WI: MBI Publishing, 2000), pp. 47–48.

Marinette Eagle Star, June 6, 1933

Don't Follow Me, I'm Lost Too!

In the early days of automobiling, spare parts and fuel were not the only things difficult to obtain: sometimes a driver had trouble merely finding the road. Before the road map became commonplace, various other pathfinding methods aided motorists. A 1910 travel guide, *Automobile Blue Book of Wisconsin*, gave detailed written instructions: "Stevens Point to Marshfield, 38 miles. Take road going west 4 miles, thence north 1 mile, thence east 1 mile to Webster. From here take road going northwest.... Condition of road: Rolling and a little hilly, but fair. Gravel and dirt road."[1]

TURN NORTH, HOTEL RACINE
Main street is the north and south street the hotel faces on, continue north. Hotel Racine offers special inducements to autoists. (See note.)

Collection of Jim Draeger

A Photographic Automobile Map traced a route from Chicago to Milwaukee using "a carefully compiled series of photographs of all turns and landmarks...along the most picturesque and pleasant route." Each photo included hand-drawn arrows indicating the correct turn, with a helpful caption, such as: "To the right [a] small cottage painted white with yellow trimmings..."[2]

Notes

1. George W. Kuehl, *Automobile Blue Book of Wisconsin: Comprising 150 Different Automobile Trips or Routes in the State of Wisconsin* (Milwaukee: The Auto Guide Publ. Co., ca. 1910), p. 127, in Turning Points in Wisconsin History.
2. *A Photographic Automobile Map: Chicago to Milwaukee* (Chicago: H. Sargent Michaels Publ. Co., ca. 1905), no. 35.

constitutional clause relegated road construction and repairs to local governments. Families living along roads offered labor and materials in lieu of tax payments, creating an odd tradition of neighborhood road repairs. Rural residents in particular were reluctant to embrace a tax-based system, but the educational efforts of the national Good Roads Movement and the accompanying declining influence of railroads resulted in approval for a 1908 constitutional amendment that created the framework for an integrated transportation system just as the automobile began to become more commonplace.

In some cases, like the Yellowstone Trail, business leaders adopted their own routes and erected way-finding aids to increase travel and bring additional commerce to their communities. The creation of the Wisconsin State Highway Commission in 1911 led to the nation's first standardized highway numbering system, established in 1918, and provided for state road aids to pay for improvements such as paving or bridge construction that would make Wisconsin a transportation leader. The Federal Aid Law of 1916 extended this coordination of highway improvements across state lines and linked Wisconsin into an emerging nationwide system of highways.

Improved roads increased long-distance travel. But as new road networks formed, highway routes presented challenges to operators of existing stations. In 1925, the federal government's Bureau of Public Roads gave formal approval to a comprehensive list of U.S. highway numbers based on a system of odd-numbered north/south roads and even-numbered east/west roads. Frank Cnare, an employee of the Wisconsin Highway Department, was responsible for the design of the now-familiar white shield with black lettering adopted in 1926 as uniform U.S. highway signage.

An example of Wisconsin's first standardized highway signs, ca. 1918. WHi Image ID 40274

Named Highways and Tourist Trails

Private booster groups established the first highways, creating cross-country trails from a patchwork of existing roads. Using their own colors and symbols, groups publicized their trails with guidebooks, maps, and other promotional materials. The Yellowstone Trail, referred to as "A good road from Plymouth Rock to Puget Sound" provided one of the best-known routes. It passed through Wisconsin, connecting Massachusetts to Washington via Yellowstone National Park. The yellow-marked route entered Wisconsin at Hudson, ran east to Abbotsford, turned southeast through Stevens Point to Milwaukee, and then went south along Lake Michigan before entering Illinois.[1]

Even after a federal highway system supplanted the trails, the naming of routes continued. Local chambers of commerce worked together in the late 1920s to create the Lucky 13, billed as "The motorists Indian trail through Wisconsin." The route cut north to south from Superior to Beloit along State Highway 13 and was promoted by a "Miss Lucky 13" through the 1960s.[2]

Collection of Jim Draeger

Notes

1. "National Roads and Road Markings" in *Wisconsin History Explorer;* Alice A. Ridge and John Wm. Ridge, *Introducing the Yellowstone Trail: A Good Road from Plymouth Rock to Puget Sound, 1912–1930* (Altoona, WI: Yellowstone Trail Publishers, 2000).
2. "Lucky 13 Boosters, Tired but Happy, Complete Tour," *Wisconsin Rapids Daily Tribune,* May 6, 1929. For more information, visit www.wisconsinhistory.org.

These developments signaled that the age of interstate auto travel had arrived. Increasingly, gas stations served travelers, which caused immediate changes in station design and placement. A *Wisconsin State Journal* article noted that a new 1924 Madison station "shows the new trend in placing these stations on the routes of tourist travel. Conveniences in the station, such as rest rooms, free air and water, crank case service, greasing rack, and spacious driveways, all illustrate the service which these stations are rendering motorists from Madison, as well as those from California, New York and any other place imaginable."[7]

We've Had Our Fill

Neighborhood Opposition and the Beautiful Station

Health and safety concerns resulted in additional regulation of gas stations. The filling station, a special-purpose building type designed exclusively to sell gasoline, came into favor. People historically used the term "filling station" to refer to those stations that pumped gas but did not have service bays. The filling station was commonly a diminutive one-story freestanding building, seldom containing more than one or two rooms. Built of brick, stone, terra-cotta, or wood, these stations quickly became ubiquitous along our streets and highways.

Filling stations became the flash point in a vigorous public debate on community development and aesthetics in the emerging auto age. Where mass-transit systems once

Numbering the Highways

In 1911, the newly created Wisconsin State Highway Commission began to improve and expand state roads and supervise the distribution of local highway funds provided by the new State Aid law. In 1916, the federal government allocated highway funds that allowed Wisconsin to develop its State Trunk Highway system, beginning in 1917.

Wisconsin recognized the need for a coherent system of highway signs. Prior to this, crossroads often featured a confusing jumble of colored markers—or no signs at all. After surveying other states, the engineers of the Highway Commission concluded that no satisfactory system existed, and in 1917 they originated the idea of numbered routes that would be adopted by the federal government in 1925. Each county prepared its own inverted triangle signs with the route number and the words "State Trunk Highway." The new signs appeared on every highway literally overnight, causing some surprise to Wisconsin residents upon their statewide unveiling on the morning of June 17, 1918.[1]

Notes

1. M. W. Torkelson, "State Highway Commission," *Wisconsin Blue Book*, 1923, pp. 177–189; "Wisconsin State Highway Work," *Wisconsin Blue Book*, 1919, pp. 275–279. For more information, visit www.wisconsinhistory.org.

dictated the location of commercial services, forcing development into compact nodes often near depots and at the ends of streetcar lines, the automobile created a new spatial order, determined by convenience and opportunity. Automobiles reduced apparent distances and allowed for sprawling commercial development, which could occur nearly anywhere along streets with high-traffic volumes. Wide boulevards that had been desirable residential locations for the nineteenth-century upper class drew gas retailers in the early twentieth century, who razed house sites for gas stations. Stations also occupied a transitional area between commercial nodes and residential neighborhoods, and builders often plunked down new stations on corner lots at conspicuous and prominent intersections.

Considered eyesores and abominations by many, gas stations interrupted the continuity of residential streetscapes. J. F. Kuntz captured public sentiment in an August 1922 *American City* magazine article:

> A casual survey of any of our large cities or small towns leads to the conclusion that many [gas station] buildings of more or less prominence have apparently been

Touring with Brownie and the Poor Cuss

As the automobile's popularity surged in the 1910s, auto touring became news. Daily or weekly columns appeared that described the adventures and hardships of traveling by car. *Milwaukee Journal* sportswriter William "Brownie" Roland turned his attention to cars sometime around 1915. Between 1915 and 1920, Roland wrote an advice column for motorists, which included descriptions of day-trip routes for the Milwaukee area.

By the 1920s, Roland's excursions had grown into monthlong odysseys of several thousand miles as he went on annual inspection tours of Wisconsin's highways and byways. Readers followed his progress through a daily log written in the voice of "Poor Cuss," Roland's reluctant, dialect-speaking travel companion. The adventure repeated every year through the 1920s but came to an end in the 1930s. The demise of his column signaled the end of a wildcat era of auto travel; state and federal highways, reliable autos, and increasing numbers of motorists had made auto touring commonplace.

A 1922 Oldsmobile ad promoting Brownie's annual tour of Wisconsin. *Milwaukee Journal,* May 14, 1922

designed by the hapless victims of some especially conspicuous form of mental aberration.... Public-spirited citizens, working through civic clubs and city planning commissions can arouse a spirit for cooperation and make an appeal to local pride that will result in a better conception of individual responsibility by each and every property owner.[8]

The intrusion of a gas station into an existing residential street often signaled the beginning of its redevelopment: As authors John Jakle and Keith A. Sculle point out in *The Gas Station in America*, these buildings were essentially pioneers of the commercial strip, for other types of freestanding, auto-centered commercial uses followed gas stations. In 1927, a *Capital Times* reporter wistfully reported the removal of five stately elms and what was believed to be Madison's oldest house to make way for a new Texaco station.[9] The correspondent noted that the station was the fifth gas station built in three blocks of University Avenue—not counting three curbside pumps.

Communities often objected as old buildings such as this one (at right)—purported, in 1927, to be the oldest standing building in Madison at that time—were razed to make room for gas stations (below).

WHi Image ID 6361

WHi Image ID 6367

As gas stations gnawed away at the nineteenth-century fabric of cities, dissatisfaction grew. Citizens pushed back, demanding better aesthetics and stronger regulation of gas stations. Gas retailers also fought against the growing public perception of their business as ugly, dirty work that drew seedy, shifty-eyed opportunists who were eager to make a quick buck.

This domestic station, part of the Green Bay chain owned by Henry Barkhausen, fits nicely into its neighborhood. WHi Image ID 40862

Architects stepped up and began offering aesthetic and functional gas station designs. Milwaukee architect Alexander Guth wrote a July 1926 article in *Architectural Forum*, a professional journal, noting that the gas station "is of such recent 'invention' that it has no background and consequently nothing to inspire either the sentimentalist or the politician."[10] Consequently, many early stations were designed as diminutive houses, conceived to reduce resistance to the establishment of gas stations in residential areas by blending them into their backgrounds. Typical designs were demure and modest, symbolic of the linkage between the automobile and the acceleration of suburban culture caused by its introduction.

The aesthetics of early filling stations usually borrowed from the Craftsman, Colonial Revival, or Tudor Revival styles. The form was a downsized version of a typical one-story bungalow or cottage. Builders used wire-cut brick and stucco—materials with residential connotations—while designers incorporated leaded-glass windows, arched doors, and window boxes, consciously wrapping the station in the symbols of domesticity.

The elaborate Tudor Revival–style Spindler station in Manitowoc. Collection of Mark Speltz

Architects of the 1920s believed that commercial enterprises of all types could bring trade through architecturally elaborate designs that appealed to status-conscious consumers. Guth argued that keen rivalry and business competition required that oil companies build attractive buildings, pointing to Arabic mosques, Norman castles, and Flemish towers as examples of higher artistic values. Although rare today, in the 1920s, many Wisconsin cities boasted showplace gas stations. Guth pointed to a number of architecturally distinguished stations such as the pagodas of Wadhams Oil in eastern Wisconsin to illustrate his contention that a visually appealing station should earn higher profits.

The Tudor Revival–style Spindler Filling and Service Station in Manitowoc illustrates how Guth and other architects visualized stations almost as romantic Victorian follies. Its elaborately patterned masonry, decorative half-timbering, sweeping roofline, and domestic appearance formed a composition that might sit harmoniously in any upscale suburb of the period. A broad expanse of lawn, landscaped with spruce trees and flagstone walks, completes the illusion of domestic fantasy. Guth noted that "were it not for the tall, whip-like pumps...this amusing little building, designed to shelter the dispenser of gas and oil, as well as provide a restroom for women travelers, would seem to be a bit of stage setting from the 'Wizard of Oz' or the 'Gingerbread Man.'"[11]

The Second-Most Beautiful Gas Station

In 1949, Shell Oil tore down an old filling station to build a modernized service station at the corner of State and Gorham streets in Madison. That station was once considered the second-most beautiful in America.

Built in 1924 by the Pennsylvania Oil Company (Pennco) to resemble a castle, the picturesque station was surrounded by eight gas pumps on individual islands and featured a large tower on one side. At night, the tower glowed with indirect lighting from fixtures hidden in ornamental stones. A 1926 contest from a gasoline trade journal judged the State Street castle to be second in beauty only to a California station with extensive landscaping.

By the 1940s, however, many of the pumps had been removed to make space for service equipment and storage, and the beautiful station was seen as old-fashioned and out of date.[1] Today, there are no gas stations on State Street, which prohibited automobile traffic beginning in the 1970s.

Notes

1. "Once 'Second Most Beautiful,' State St. Station's Torn Down," *Wisconsin State Journal*, June 26, 1949; "Prize-winning Station," *Wisconsin State Journal*, December 31, 1926.

Courtesy of O. J. Thompto

In the minds of 1920s architects, good station design—that which used the symbolic power of domestic and civic imagery—was equated with civility. Guth even downplays the need for any commercial identity, stating, "In the case of this building no red or green painted oil pump on the edge of the sidewalk is needed to catch the eye of the motorist. No one passing by at less than 40 miles an hour could fail to notice this unusual bit of architecture."[12] For Guth, the unwitting motorist would be as dumbstruck as Dorothy thrust into the splendor of Oz and, gobsmacked by the station's beauty, feel powerless to pass and compelled to return.

Branded

Standard Designs and Corporate Identity

Larger oil companies also joined the fight for good station design through the adoption of design standards for stations in their retail chains. The Pure Oil Company was a pioneer in the establishment of an integrated corporate image that permeated all aspects of the company's gasoline retailing. Pure Oil branded every part of its business—from matchbooks and road maps to stationery and signage, including the station itself—with a consistent design and color scheme. Influenced by the discipline of consumer psychology emerging in the mid-1920s, Pure Oil hired Carl A. Petersen to create a standardized cottage-style station design featuring a bright blue tiled gable roof atop a building painted white with blue highlights. Two tall end chimneys, copper hoods over the windows and doors, shutters, and a flower box completed the design.

Architect Carl A. Petersen chose to have his Pure Oil cottage-style station patented. Few gas station designers sought this right. U.S. Patent D 77857

Petersen chose the house form in part to appease discontent in residential neighborhoods but also because it carried a powerful psychological message, associating the gas station with strong emotional feelings of home and family, belonging and tradition. In 1928, the Pure Oil Company patented its "cottage" design and, over the next decade, erected hundreds of nearly identical stations across the country.[13] Petersen created variations to accommodate different-size lots and locations. Freitag's Pure Oil in Monroe (see page 72) is an example of the small station with attached service bay, while the company scaled Henry Ott's station in La Crosse (see page 68) to a more urban market. At its grand reopening in 1937, Ott advertised his station as a "shopping center" for motorists.

Due to the specific considerations of time and place, Pure Oil stations were not truly identical; nevertheless, this movement toward a standardized image influenced later designs.

Taking Credit

Credit existed long before the invention of the credit card. In pre-twentieth-century America, country stores extended credit to local farmers awaiting the harvest, and merchants and manufacturers offered installment plans for their more expensive items. The "charge card" came into being as retailers expanded and could no longer know all their customers personally. Merchants needed a system to recognize customers with charge accounts, and so they began to issue paper cards with the customer's name and account number.

WHS Museum 2002.256.5 #1

WHS Museum 2002.256.7 #2

The charge card became especially important to oil companies. Rapid expansion in the 1910s and 1920s allowed companies to cover large geographic regions. Texaco, for example, issued its first credit cards in 1914,[1] and other companies began similar programs around the same time. The standardized card identified customers at any station, anywhere. Most important, credit cards encouraged customer loyalty to the brand, rather than the station, so that travelers would stick with the company while on the road.

Oil companies and other merchants faced stiff competition after the advent of the Diners Club card in 1950 (a third-party-issued card that customers could use at a variety of businesses) and the later introduction of the modern credit card.

Notes

1. "Texaco Heritage: Timeline: 1912–1927: Stations," www.texaco.com/heritage/texaco_heritage.html.

The importance of Pure Oil's approach was its conception of station design as architectural packaging that contributed to a consistent and an easily identifiable image. Pure Oil exemplified the emergence of modern corporate marketing strategies, which during the next decade transformed gas retailing and the stations themselves.

The pagoda-inspired stations of Wadhams Oil Company are a regional example of this same phenomenon. A major concern of early gas retailers was to find a way to distinguish their gasoline from the competitors' products. Oil companies, like Wadhams, were attempting to expand into new markets, but because consistent consumer loyalty had not yet been established, they were eager to find ways to compete on a basis other than price. Creating an identifiable image for their chain translated into easy product recognition.

In the mid-1910s, Wadhams, an emerging regional gas chain, approached Alexander C. Eschweiler, a leading Milwaukee architect, to create an indelible gas station design.

Alexander C. Eschweiler, Wadhams architect and designer of the pagoda-style station. **WHi Image ID 57260**

Eschweiler's pagoda design played off public fascination with travel and exotica. **Collection of Jim Draeger**

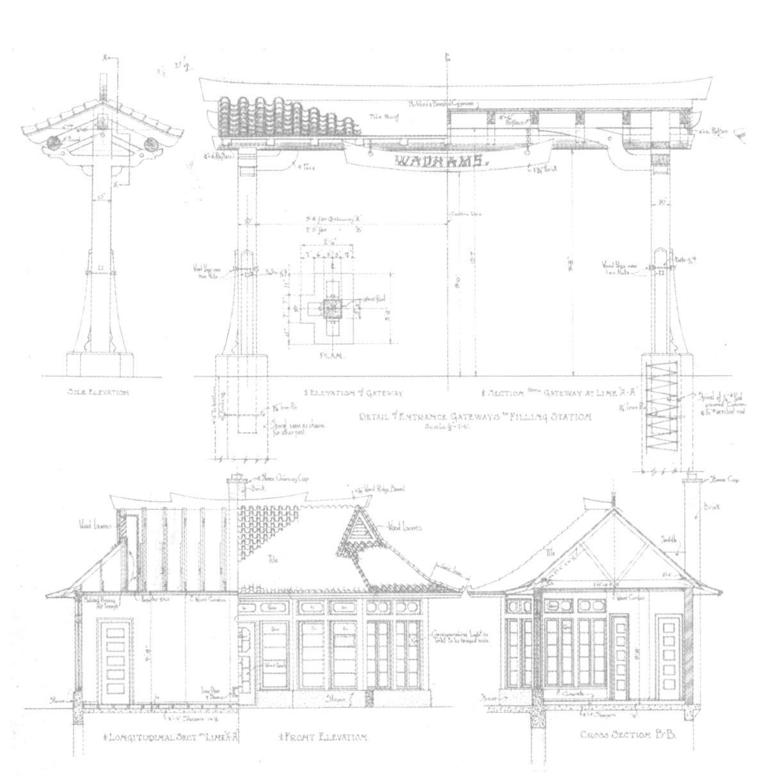

Eschweiler's elevation and cross section drawings for a Milwaukee Wadhams station. **Milwaukee Architectural Archives, Milwaukee Public Library**

A pagoda-style Wadhams station, featuring an extraordinarily elaborate tower. **Courtesy of Milwaukee County Historical Society**

Eschweiler wedded yearnings for roadside adventures made possible by the auto with a deep-seated public fascination with the exotica of far-off places. He chose a Japanese pagoda design, which, while novel, was yet recognizable due to the interest in Japanese culture sparked, in part, by a series of world's fairs that included Japanese pavilions. Eschweiler's genius was to skillfully marry the ornate and exotic three-dimensional billboard of a roof to a functionalist and modernist glass box base, creating an attention-getting aesthetic design that was also practical. Wadhams pagodas became destinations themselves, drawing repeat traffic with their whimsical and fantastic appearances. The company built more than one hundred of these striking stations between 1917 and 1930. Wadhams' iconographic stations greatly influenced commercial strip design and are the precursors of the bold designs of modern fast-food architecture.

Eye-grabbing gas station designs were a trend during the early twentieth century. Novelty architecture like the Wadhams pagoda competed with windmills, wigwams, and other fantastical forms. The station at Phil's Lake Nokomis Resort in Heafford Junction (see page 150) relied on the visual incongruity of the windmill in the wilds of northern Wisconsin to pull travelers off

Are We There Yet?

During the mid-twentieth century, one of America's most recognizable marketing devices was the free gas station road map. Gulf Oil distributed the first free road maps in Ohio in 1913; it expanded the program into the northeastern states the next year. Recognizing a good idea, other big oil companies and several map publishers, including Rand McNally and Company, began collaborating on maps in the 1920s. These early maps did not fully evolve until Wisconsin (and then the rest of the country) created numbered highway systems, which made the task of road mapping considerably easier.

From the beginning, colorful and sumptuous road maps romanticized the open road and encouraged travel while promoting the oil company at the same time. Cartography evolved alongside the road map, featuring increasingly sophisticated symbols and color codes. For more than fifty years, the free road map was an indispensable feature of every service station, until the oil shortages and declining profits of the 1970s compelled oil companies to cut back on free handouts. Today, the cover graphics are merely utilitarian—and the maps are no longer free.[1]

Northwoods Petroleum Museum, photo by Joel Heiman

Notes

1. Douglas Yorke, John Margolies, and Eric Baker, *Hitting the Road: The Art of the American Road Map* (San Francisco: Chronicle Books, 1996), pp. 114–119.

the road. Others made use of local materials to capture the irresistible essence of place, like Harry Klippel's log cabin station south of Hazelhurst (see page 148). Its rustic design suggested to tourists that their vacation began at the gas pump. Station designs were not accidental, and each reflected its owner's attempt to appeal to a certain consumer market.

This stunning teepee station served tourists in Weyauwega.
WHi Image ID 57214

Another approach to station design was to build quick, cheap, and easy. In a competitive marketplace, where profitable locations were difficult to predict, many owners opted to save investment capital and construct inexpensive buildings to quickly establish territory and minimize start-up costs. Many owners, such as Felix Ohrlein in Prairie du Sac (see page 76), chose to buy prefabricated stations from companies such as the Madison-based Trachte Brothers Company. The brothers had patented a corrugated steel–rolling machine that they used to produce water tanks. After George Trachte erected a metal garage for his new Dodge in 1919, they somewhat accidentally found their way into the prefabricated building business. The Trachtes began producing bolt-together metal buildings that found a variety of uses, including garages and gas stations. A key to the structures' success was a modular approach to design, which allowed each building to be easily lengthened or widened to meet nearly any specification.

Long-lived gas station builder Steel King got its start in Milwaukee in 1926, creating automobile garages that bore a striking resemblance to Trachte's metal buildings. Founder Walter C. Junkerman spotted a need for quick and cheap auto-related structures in a booming market and, in 1929, stepped into the commercial building business, constructing roadside stands, ticket booths, small stores and offices, and gas stations. Unlike the Trachte Brothers Company, Steel King found a major niche in station erection. Steel King subcontracted fabrication to Milwaukee manufacturers, such as Standard Sheet Metal, while keeping an inventory of overhead doors and windows and other standardized station components. The company based its early success on its ability to adapt, accommodate, and change.

The fanciful pump island canopy at the now demolished Badger Country Station in Antigo enticed travelers. Photo by Jim Draeger

Trachte Brothers Company

Trachte Steel Filling Stations

THE Filling Station offers the man seeking a business of his own a greater opportunity than the grocery store ever did. The Trachte Portable Steel Filling Station has been tested by thorough experience for utility, economy, durability and beauty and has not been found wanting. A practical service station in which the capital investment is cut to a minimum without sacrificing desirable essentials. Economical, portable, durable, attractive.

Office 16′ x 10′ x 10′ wall. 16′ x 14′ canopy. 1 No. GP 37 and 1 No. WP 2466 door. 3 No. 33-161 windows.

Page sixteen

The Trachte Brothers' prefabricated steel buildings made cheap, fast, and easy-to-erect stations. Collection of Jim Draeger

Working in the "Luberatory"

The Development of Effective Gas Station Layouts

The plot plans and layouts of early stations were casual and not systematically defined by regulation or trade practice. Builders based arrangements on convenience and necessary adaptations to the limitations of haphazard building sites. By the mid-1920s, a standardized approach emerged for the design of small filling stations, which became archetypical of this phase of station design. Smaller stations consisted largely of an "operator's room" and an adjacent concrete "pump island."

Higher-performance engines introduced in the 1920s burned a significant amount of oil—as much as a quart every 250 miles—making the provision of motor oil in a wide variety of blends a major part of filling station operation. Even the smallest stations provided an oil room, sometimes in the basement, where operators stored bulk oil and dispensed it by a hand-cranked pump called a "lubester." Before the invention of the prefilled oilcan, the so-called luberatory held drums of motor oil. Occasionally, companies relegated the oil room to a separate structure immediately adjacent to the station, likely because of oil's odor and flammability. These spaces became largely outmoded with the adoption of the prefilled oilcan.

Pump-island canopies, presumably introduced for the comfort of patrons leaving their cars to enter the station, were a much-discussed topic in station design, but they were much

Prior to the development of the car hoist, grease monkeys serviced autos in pits like this version (to the left of the station, with the white curbs) in Green Bay. Courtesy of UWM Libraries, Archives Department, UWM Mss 131, Box 9, F 2 #44091

Before the invention of the familiar metal quart oil can, oil was hand measured and dispensed using glass or metal containers like these. WHS Museum 1983.291.2E (bottle), WHS Museum 1978.396.5 (can)

Until large service bays became standard, small stations, like this Milwaukee one, often installed their hoists outdoors. Courtesy of UWM Libraries, Archives Department, UWM Mss 131, Box 9, F 2 #44117

more practical for the pump jockeys standing on the pump island in all weather. Canopies were a significant additional construction expense, so their commonplace appearance is a testimony to their usefulness. However, a canopy created an aesthetic problem in station design. It needed to be tall enough to accommodate the largest truck and strong enough to span the space between the station and the pumps. Due to its large scale, a canopy was difficult to treat architecturally. Most designers conceived the canopy as an amalgam of porch and the Victorian-era porte cochere. They often detailed canopy supports in a bungalow fashion with a squat square pier and a narrower post or column.

Filling stations also provided simple repairs and servicing such as oil changes and lubrication of vehicle joints. Station layouts sometimes included either an outdoor "grease pit" or an elevated platform for seasonal auto servicing in lieu of a service bay. Pits were preferred due to the dangers of running a car off the ramp of an elevated platform. An attendant scrambled up and down a ladder placed at the far end of the pit, giving rise to the term "grease monkey."

Marketing was done mostly on a local level in the filling-station era. While an important part of retailing, there was little deliberate and studied strategy. Guth's *Architectural Forum* article, for example, contains no mention of signage or advertising in his discussion of station design. Various oil companies provided porcelain enamel signs in a hodgepodge of sizes, shapes, and forms, which retailers nailed onto their buildings, leaned against the walls, or strung along the grassy median. Retailers also improvised handmade signs; oilcan sculptures depicting animals, windmills, people, and miniature gas stations; and other whimsical attention getters in an attempt to be noticed along an increasingly busy and crowded roadside.

This oil-can dog at the Hill Service Station in Ripon joined oil-can men and an oil-can windmill in beckoning customers. Courtesy of Craig Tebon

Gas Station Bandits

Since their earliest days, filling stations have always been prime targets for holdups and thieves. Following are some examples from Wisconsin newspapers, ranging from the humorous to the dangerous.

★ ***Daring:*** Janesville, 1923. A bold robber, not bothering with a mask or disguise, walked into a Standard Oil station early on a Monday morning and cleaned the safe of Sunday's entire profit: four hundred dollars.[1]

★ ***Repeat Offenders:*** Eau Claire, 1939. Two gunmen stole a car in Winona, Minnesota, and then robbed two Eau Claire gas stations in succession. After shooting the second station's attendant in his back, they fled the scene.[2]

★ ***Bad Luck:*** Madison, 1924. A gas station robber was foiled when he could not get the cash drawer open.[3]

★ ***Really Bad Luck:*** Burlington, 1930. Four young men were attempting to pry open a pump to steal a tank of gasoline. Their disturbance created an electric spark—which caused an explosion that knocked them off their feet and brought the police running.[4]

★ ***Déjà Vu:*** Madison, 1930. The same Standard Oil station was robbed three times in one week.[5]

★ ***Small Change:*** Menasha, 1939. An armed bandit held up a filling station but, unfortunately for him, found only seven dollars in the cash register.[6]

★ ***Talked Out of It:*** Kenosha, 1930. A young would-be robber demanded that the station owner "stick 'em up." When the owner reminded the kid that "people get arrested for that kind of thing," the kid looked "crestfallen" and then ran away.[7]

★ ***Young Felons:*** Appleton, 1927. Two young boys, ages eleven and thirteen, escaped from a Milwaukee reform school (to which they had been sentenced only two weeks previously for robbing a filling station), held up an Appleton Deep Rock station, and menaced a motorist with stolen hunting knives before the police caught up with them.[8]

★ ***Baby Burglaries:*** Neenah, 1940. Three boys were suspected of stealing sixty-five pennies, a flashlight, a pocketknife, and $1.50 in soda and candy from two area filling stations. The boys gained entrance to the stations in the night through their back windows.[9]

★ ***Foiled:*** Madison, 1937. Pulling his car into a gas station, a robber pointed a pistol at the attendant who came over. The attendant ran for the station and slammed the door just in time to stop the man's bullet, foiling the robbery.[10]

Notes

1. "$400 Stolen in Daylight Holdup of 'Gas' Station," *Janesville Daily Gazette*, June 30, 1923.
2. "Eau Claire Gas Station Worker Shot in Holdup," *La Crosse Tribune and Leader-Press*, January 18, 1939.
3. "Burglar Foiled," *Capital Times*, August 11, 1924.
4. "Explosion of Service Tank Gets Thieves," *Burlington Standard Democrat*, September 5, 1930.
5. "Local News," *Sheboygan Press*, October 28, 1930.
6. "Bandit Holds Up Filling Station," *Appleton Post-Crescent*, March 4, 1939.
7. "Youthful Bandit Frightened Away," *Sheboygan Press*, August 11, 1930.
8. "Young Gas Station Thieves Caught as They Pass Police," *Appleton Post-Crescent*, October 1, 1927.
9. "Youths Questioned in Gas Station Thefts," *Appleton Post-Crescent*, August 29, 1940.
10. "Masked Robber Fires at Gas Station Man Who Foils Robbery," *Oshkosh Northwestern*, December 20, 1937.

Powder Puffs and Petrol

Class, Gender, and Station Design

Class and gender distinctions were a conspicuous part of station design in the mid-1920s. As odd as the fantasy stations seem to our modern eye, oil companies grounded their design in an understanding that customers in this period were largely upscale, the automobile mainly a prized plaything of the rich. The lavishness of Spindler's Tudor Revival–style station makes more sense when considering the lifestyles and cultural expectations of those wealthy enough to own Packards, Buicks, Cadillacs, and other luxury cars of the period.

Women's history texts, such as Virginia Scharff's *Taking the Wheel: Women and the Coming of the Motor Age*, have explored the transformative role that autos played in the women's movement in the early twentieth century. Gas retailers saw a potential market in the growing number of affluent women motorists who were taking to the road on their own, enjoying unprecedented independent mobility away from their traditional sphere in the home. The Powder Puff station of Waupun, designed by Green Bay architects Foeller, Schober, and Stephenson, made a direct appeal to female motorists. According to *The Master Builder* magazine:

The charming Powder Puff station in Waupun lured the increasingly common female driver. ***The Master Builder*, June 1927**

> Oil companies are beginning to realize that it is the station unique in design and cozy and homelike in appearance that will quickly draw the trade of the passing motorist. This is especially true today when so many women are driving cars.... The men will not realize just why they are attracted to the newer type of filling station, while the women are keen to sense the reason.[14]

Well-heeled women could also delight in the "powder puff" room that gave this station its name. Popular in upscale establishments of the period, the powder puff room was a sitting room where ladies could touch up their makeup and socialize beyond men's gazes. Furnished with wicker chairs, a settee, and a reading table and accented with elaborate draperies and a tapestry

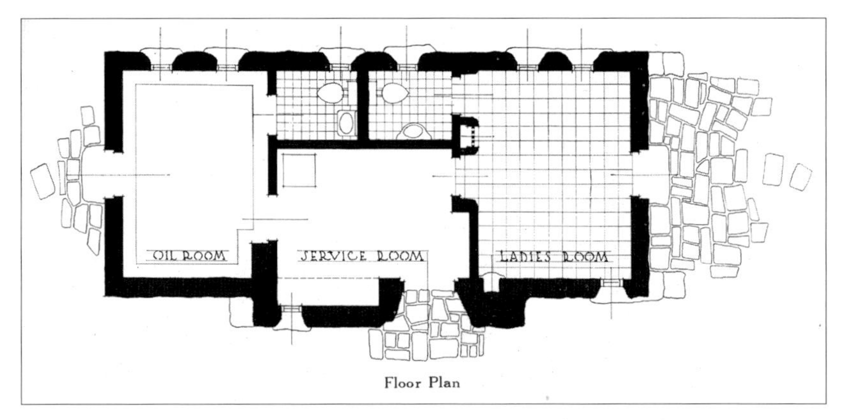

The Spindler station floor plan: The ladies' room takes up a large percentage of the building's footprint. ***Architectural Forum,*** **July 1926**

rug, this anteroom to the ladies' restroom occupied more than a third of the station's interior and signaled an understanding of the stereotypical gender preferences and roles of its customers.

The location of restrooms and their relationship to other station spaces also signaled gender differences. Access to the women's room was almost exclusively via a door placed inconspicuously on the side of the building, while the men's room was accessible from inside. Men shared a restroom near the office area with station attendants (presumed to be male), signaling that companies saw the business portion of the interior as an exclusively male space. Positioning the men's restroom off the salesroom not only saved the cost of a separate restroom for the attendant but also encouraged "point-of-purchase" sales, reflecting the perception that auto goods were masculine products.

The Black Earth Pennco station had its ladies' room entrance outside the station, as was typical in the 1920s. WHi Image ID 40436

White Gloves and Clean Bathrooms

Women became more frequent drivers in the 1920s and 1930s, and companies responded with new advertising and business approaches. One notable change was in the service station restroom. As stations proliferated in the 1920s, consumers began to have a choice among businesses, and thus aesthetics and quality of services began to play a larger role in attracting and keeping customers. This led to landscaped English Cottage–style stations and well-equipped, separate restrooms for women.

In the late 1930s and 1940s, companies took their clean bathroom campaign to a higher level. In 1938, Shell Oil collaborated with *Good Housekeeping* magazine to put a "Seal of Approval" on their restrooms, and Texaco began its "White Patrol"—sending women inspectors to certify their "Registered Restrooms" with a green-and-white sign. Phillips Petroleum Company created a corps of "Highway Hostesses," while trade journals such as *National Petroleum News* stressed to all station managers the importance of clean facilities.[1] The last of the clean-bathroom campaigns, Union Oil's "Sparkle Corp," was phased out in the early 1960s, and service station facilities reverted to their natural state: dirty.[2]

Collection of Jim Draeger

Notes

1. Susan Spellman, "All the Comforts of Home: The Domestication of the Service Station Industry, 1920–1940," *The Journal of Popular Culture* 37, no. 3 (2004): pp. 463–477.
2. John Margolies, *Pump and Circumstance* (Boston: Little, Brown and Company, Bullfinch Press,1993), p. 105.

Booming Business
The Regulation of Gas Stations

The rapid proliferation of gas stations in the 1920s and 1930s increased concern about injuries and accidents. A 1933 incident at a Pennsylvania Oil Company station in Madison illustrates the public-safety issues behind expanded regulations. On June 16, a tremendous explosion demolished the station. Flying debris lacerated and bruised the attendant, Clifford Penn, and his brother Harry, who had dropped by for a chat. The blast blew Henry Callahan, an unlucky pedestrian, into the street. A witness stated:

> I saw the gasoline pumps tossed up into the air, and then the concrete was heaved up and some of it turned right upside down. I started to run toward the station, and I saw the walls sort of burst out. Cliff was standing near the doorway, and I saw him crumpling up under the wall as it dropped. The roof seemed to hang in the air for a minute and then it dropped down to the ground. I was afraid Cliff was dead.[15]

It was Madison's second station explosion of the year. Inspectors traced the cause to an accumulation of gas vapors, which had gathered in the abandoned basement of the building that had existed on the site previously. To save money, workers had filled the foundation with gravel and constructed the station on top. Vapors accumulated in the porous space and, ignited by a short in faulty wiring, caused the explosion. The incident underscored the need for stringent regulatory controls.

The explosion of this Pennco station rocked Madison's Park Street the morning of June 16, 1933. WHi Image ID 17254

Because many cities did not require building permits or regulate station design, the Industrial Commission of Wisconsin oversaw the construction of gas stations and enforced state building codes. Beginning in 1918, the commission had exercised authority over auto garages; concerns about the proliferation of gas stations in the late 1920s resulted in an expansion of authority in 1931. The commission's building inspectors began carefully and doggedly policing the construction of stations, ensuring public safety.

When Leo Salkowski built his Wadhams station in 1931 (see page 108), he could not have expected that almost five years later he would still be under the steely gaze of Charles Wheeler, regional inspector for the commission. Salkowski's mistake was to borrow blueprints from a station owner in his hometown of Chicago and erect a station without proper approval in his new hometown of Kewaunee. Salkowski's plans contained a number of defects that did not comply with detailed Wisconsin requirements.

Wheeler chastised Kewaunee's mayor and the contractor, Albrecht Manufacturing Company, for

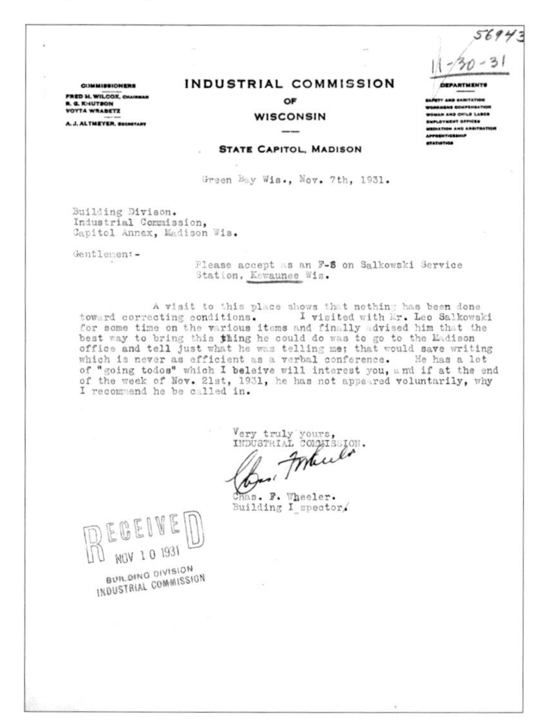

56943

11-30-31

COMMISSIONERS
FRED M. WILCOX, CHAIRMAN
R. G. KNUTSON
VOYTA WRABETZ
A. J. ALTMEYER, SECRETARY

INDUSTRIAL COMMISSION
OF
WISCONSIN

STATE CAPITOL, MADISON

DEPARTMENTS
SAFETY AND SANITATION
WORKMENS COMPENSATION
WOMAN AND CHILD LABOR
EMPLOYMENT OFFICES
MEDIATION AND ARBITRATION
APPRENTICESHIP
STATISTICS

Green Bay Wis., Nov. 7th, 1931.

Building Divison.
Industrial Commission,
Capitol Annex, Madison Wis.

Gentlemen:-

Please accept as an F-8 on Salkowski Service Station, Kewaunee Wis.

A visit to this place shows that nothing has been done toward correcting conditions. I visited with Mr. Leo Salkowski for some time on the various items and finally advised him that the best way to bring this thing he could do was to go to the Madison office and tell just what he was telling me; that would save writing which is never as efficient as a verbal conference. He has a lot of "going todos" which I beleive will interest you, and if at the end of the week of Nov. 21st, 1931, he has not appeared voluntarily, why I recommend he be called in.

Very truly yours,
INDUSTRIAL COMMISSION.

Chas. F. Wheeler.
Building I_spector.

RECEIVED
NOV 10 1931
BUILDING DIVISION
INDUSTRIAL COMMISSION

Beginning in the 1930s, the Industrial Commission of Wisconsin enforced strict rules for the building of service stations. WHS Series 2284, Box 297

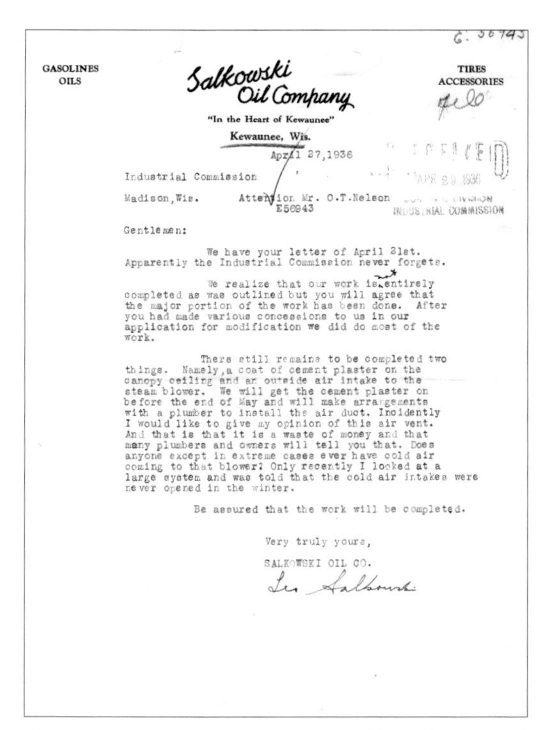

GASOLINES
OILS

Salkowski Oil Company

"In the Heart of Kewaunee"

Kewaunee, Wis.

TIRES
ACCESSORIES

April 27,1936

Industrial Commission

Madison, Wis. Attention Mr. O.T.Nelson
E56943

Gentlemen:

We have your letter of April 21st. Apparently the Industrial Commission never forgets.

We realize that our work is not entirely completed as was outlined but you will agree that the major portion of the work has been done. After you had made various concessions to us in our application for modification we did do most of the work.

There still remains to be completed two things. Namely, a coat of cement plaster on the canopy ceiling and an outside air intake to the steam blower. We will get the cement plaster on before the end of May and will make arrangements with a plumber to install the air duct. Incidently I would like to give my opinion of this air vent. And that is that it is a waste of money and that many plumbers and owners will tell you that. Does anyone except in extreme cases ever have cold air coming to that blower? Only recently I looked at a large system and was told that the cold air intakes were never opened in the winter.

Be assured that the work will be completed.

Very truly yours,

SALKOWSKI OIL CO.

Leo Salkowski

Kewaunee station owner Leo Salkowski argued back and forth with the Industrial Commission for nearly five years over his station's noncompliance with regulations. WHS Series 2284, Box 297

their lack of oversight, but it was Salkowski who was responsible for making significant construction changes to conform to state codes. Salkowski pleaded ignorance; he cited the hard times caused by the Depression, asked character witnesses to write the commission, stalled, and ignored Wheeler's repeated demands in an attempt to avoid costly design changes. Wheeler listened and negotiated conditional changes, but he never wavered from his position that building modifications were required. Finally, in April 1936, Salkowski conceded to the changes, stating, "Apparently the Industrial Commission never forgets."[16]

With the 1931 reforms, the Industrial Commission of Wisconsin effected sweeping changes in station construction. Through its regulatory powers, it imposed a single standard upon all of the state's stations; it also placed station design firmly in the hands of professional architects and gas station building manufacturers and suppliers. Independent station owners and corporations alike needed to satisfy the commission's requirements, resulting in a consistent approach to design necessitated by rules and regulations.

The commission also used its authority to require the removal of antiquated and dangerous equipment, forcing the renovation of aging stations. When a ten-year-old La Crosse station received a makeover in 1937 by the

The La Crosse Pure Oil station before (top) and after (bottom) it was remodeled in 1937 to reflect the cottage-style corporate brand. WHi Image ID 45925 (top), WHi Image ID 45928 (bottom)

Pure Oil Company to conform its design to the corporation's standard, the commission insisted that the company remove the old service pit as well. Pure Oil argued to no avail that the work was purely cosmetic, consisting of a "face-lifting" that did not involve the service bays. C. J. Cadell, regional inspector for the commission, noted in the case file that Pure Oil admitted spending nearly ten thousand dollars on the makeover, so the commission continued to pressure Pure Oil, which reluctantly complied.[17] Through this type of careful review and studious enforcement, the commission advanced the craft and practice of station design.

Cities, too, regulated gas stations. Concerned by the unbridled growth in the number of gas stations in the 1920s and 1930s, as well as the effects of too much competition on local jobs and wages, cities passed ordinances controlling the design and location of stations. In 1939, Stoughton expanded its existing ban on curbside pumps to place strict limits on the number of gas stations. In a two-cigar meeting, Alderman Herman Gjertson countered free-enterprise arguments by asserting that the construction of many stations along Main Street resulted in depreciating property values for home owners who found themselves next door to a new station. Not surprisingly, owners of existing stations supported the measure—including Alderman Harry Chapin, a station owner who in his enlightened self-interest voted yes. Gjertson and his colleagues prevailed, curbing the construction of new stations.[18]

Luxurious Necessity

Gas Retailing During the Depression

By the time of the stock market crash in 1929, gasoline retailing had become a mature industry. Regional and national oil companies were established and had well-defined territories. Gas stations were ubiquitous in both city and countryside, assuring a reliable supply for the motoring public. Station designs had become refined, and the domestic station form was commonplace. The essential elements—display windows, restrooms, location of gas pumps, and setback from the street—had become routine. Marketing schemes using color, logos, mottos, and standard practices were in place. The subsequent economic

This ca. 1930s pump shows the complexity of its mechanism, which now displayed the money owed as well as gallons dispensed. Courtesy of UWM Libraries, Archives Department, UWM Mss 131, Box 10, F 2

The Black Eagle service station in Madison shows the difficulty of incorporating displays of tires, batteries, and other accessories into station layouts. WHi Image ID 14726

downturn during the Depression changed the landscape of gas retailing and resulted in another cycle of innovation and modification.

As financial hardships gripped the nation, gas retailing was one of the few segments of the economy that did not dramatically shrink. People clung to their automobiles, continuing to spend on what had now become essential auto-related goods and services. In less than a decade, the auto had moved from a frivolous plaything of the rich in the early 1920s to a necessary requirement for living a modern lifestyle. Afraid to face a shrinking market as the Depression deepened, oil companies stepped up competition, seeing business expansion as a bulwark against an uncertain future. These forces resulted in a retooling of stations to meet the needs of a new age. Gas retailers focused on stimulating business through adding stations, refining marketing plans, and offering quality products, superior service, efficient operations, and a standardized, attractive, and compelling image.

This intense competition encouraged station owners to add vehicle service—once the nearly exclusive domain of auto-repair garages and viewed by many gas retailers as a dirty and troublesome sideline. The invention of the hydraulic car hoist in 1925 by Memphis, Tennessee, auto mechanic Peter Lunati made it easy to bring auto servicing indoors and eliminate the service pit. By the Depression, the addition of service bays to lure additional customers and increase ancillary sales was almost essential to survival. Gregario Gallo's in Kenosha (see page 106) and Davis and Barnard's station in Spring Green (see page 82) received service bay

Harold Smith, a University of Wisconsin football tackle, at work at a Madison Valvoline station in 1931, exemplified the friendly station attendant—a crucial contribution to a station's success.
WHi Image ID 19383

additions to their 1920s stations. Other owners demolished their earlier stations and replaced them with newer structures that included service bays. So-called super-service stations, such as Edwards Super Service in Madison (see page 112), emerged in the more populous cities. In this station, H. G. Edwards brought together hitherto separate automotive activities such as storage, car washing, tire repair, tire sales, and even twenty-four-hour servicing that was unusual for the period, creating one-stop shopping for motorists.

Collection of Jim Draeger

In the 1930s, oil companies heavily promoted customer service. Gas retailers understood that the majority of income came from repeat business. Corporations began to adopt features such as uniformed attendants and promoted clean restrooms to attract and retain customers. Attendants checked oil, cleaned windows, filled radiators, and inflated tires to create a caring image. The gas station operator became much more than a pump jockey, and the gas station more than a mere fueling depot. Loyalty to a neighborhood station was transferable to the corporation: As people traveled farther, they readily associated the experience of their neighborhood station to the larger oil company brand.

The Little Independents That Could

Clark, Pennco, and Wadhams

As gas sales declined during the Depression, oil refiners found themselves with a gas surplus. They marketed their excess to emerging independent retailers, and the number of small, start-up companies grew.

Emory T. Clark, founder of Clark Oil Company. **Courtesy of Marjorie Clark Takton**

One of Wisconsin's most successful start-ups was Clark Oil Company. Emory T. Clark's story is a classic rags-to-riches tale. When his father left his mother and five sons to support themselves, Clark dropped out of fifth grade and began a series of odd jobs to help take care of the family. A self-made man, he ran a successful construction business until a fateful day in 1932, when a client defaulted on a loan and Clark took over a tiny one-pump station at Sixtieth and Greenfield streets in West Allis. He debated whether he should pursue a career in petroleum or start a floral business, but a little coaxing from his wife drove him to expand his little station into an independent network.

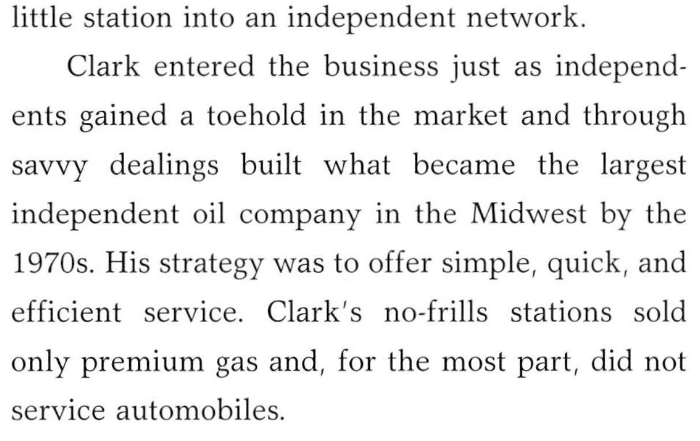

Clark entered the business just as independents gained a toehold in the market and through savvy dealings built what became the largest independent oil company in the Midwest by the 1970s. His strategy was to offer simple, quick, and efficient service. Clark's no-frills stations sold only premium gas and, for the most part, did not service automobiles.

"Independently owned" was an effective marketing strategy in the years following the Depression. **Collection of Jim Draeger**

His daughter Marjorie Clark Takton said her father always wanted Clark Oil attendants to show up at the pumps with clean hands. He policed his own stations on Sunday drives with his family: attendants who provided superior service received commendations, and those who did not uphold his standards soon heard from their station managers.

(Above and left)
Courtesy of Marjorie Clark Takton; photos by Joel Heiman

Independents built their businesses based on the personal relationship between the operator and the customer. The Madison-based independent Pennsylvania Oil Company, or Pennco, touted its advantages to customers in a 1930 marketing piece:

> Pennco is a Madison organization employing Madison people, paying Madison taxes, supporting Madison projects
>
> Pennco gives you more for your money
>
> Pennco delivers an extra measure of service[19]

The message is clear: Trust a locally owned company, which as an independent can save you money and cares more, providing you with superior service. Because owners were in close proximity to their stations, it was easy to establish a service ethic, maintain standards, and create a predictable customer experience. The major companies used marketing to instill a relationship between company and customer, but their service ethic had to be codified in formal policy and practice and enforced through corporate oversight.

Gas station attendant uniforms presented a crisp, respectable image to customers. **Courtesy of UWM Libraries, Archives Department, UWM Mss 131, Box 9, F 2 #45653**

Despite efforts in the 1920s to reform the unsavory image of gas retailing, the residual memory of the shady station operator who short-changed customers or cheated on vehicle service continued to affect the way consumers perceived gas stations. Corporations responded by promoting images of consistency, quality service, prompt attention, and clean and orderly operation. Companies carefully policed each station to ensure that their operation reinforced this market image. *Wadhams Gasoline Station Manual* provided forty-five pages of detailed policies and procedures for the station owner and attendants. It began with an extensive discussion of cleanliness:

> Anything short of absolute cleanliness is intolerable, both to the customer and the Company. The appearance of the station—the condition of the drive, the islands, the building—is the customer's first and last impression of your station. By that impression will the customer gauge his desire to return to you, and sister Wadhams Stations—or stop elsewhere.[20]

Nattily attired attendants ready to greet customers in 1940 at the grand opening of the Madison Skelly station, located in the former Edwards Super Service Station (see page 112). Courtesy of O. J. Thompto

The strongest component of this strategy was the attendant, which Wadhams referred to as "the connecting link between the Company and the public which it serves [*sic*]."[21] The company emphasized the need for a positive, courteous attitude and understood that image began with the attendant's appearance. By the 1930s, most companies required attendants to wear a uniform, guaranteeing a consistent look and image. The Wadhams manual explained the company's dress code:

> The Salesman must be in complete uniform at all times. Coveralls, cap, money changer, charge book and pencil, badge, and a clean rag constitute the uniform. Shirts with collars and ties must be worn at all times. Uniforms are to be buttoned to within one button of the neck.[22]

Gas companies paid attention to the complex interaction between the attendant and the customer, which was at the core of the customer experience. Full-service stations created a personal bond between the attendant and the customer. Wadhams emphasized a personal but professional relationship, urging attendants to "Treat all customers in accordance with uniform method as proscribed."[23] The company continually emphasized in its training materials that its employees should avoid or defuse controversy, avoid embarrassing the customer, and carry a proper deportment. They enforced adherence to company policy through a mixture of expectations and rewards. Sales quotas were established for each station and bonuses offered for exceptional performance.

Despite their importance to gas companies, the work of station attendants was difficult. They worked long hours without overtime or holiday pay in all weather until Congress passed the Fair Labor Standards Act on June 25, 1938. A 1931 U.S. Department of Labor study revealed that the average gas station employee worked six and a half days, a sixty-hour workweek. It noted that turnover was steady: the typical attendant stayed less than a year, possibly because many attendants were young men starting in the job market. The workforce at the time was overwhelmingly male, with only eight females among the nearly three thousand workers studied for the report.[24]

The station attendant was the social director of informal communities that grew up around the interactions that occurred at gas stations. Because stations were high-traffic places with many comings and goings, like nineteenth-century railroad depots, they became natural gathering places. Station stories are rife with anecdotes of these complex interactions: tales of schoolboys dropping their neckties off on the way to school or of old-timers gathering over doughnuts in the corner of the service bay next to the car hoist. The attendant served as moderator, balancing the need for a profitable and efficient workplace with the desire to create a welcoming atmosphere.

Thinking Inside the Box

The Science of Service

Competition was at the core of dramatic changes in station architecture that emerged during the depths of the Depression. Oil companies quickly jettisoned the respectable imagery of pseudo-suburban houses and civic monuments in exchange for a sleek, unadorned box-type station. People began to accept gas stations as necessary evils, and local land-use regulations and ordinances established the "gasoline alleys" of cities, reducing widespread resistance to new stations. Companies replaced the casual and intuitive approach to station design evident in the 1920s with a scientific methodology to determine which factors increased profitability. The newly emerging discipline of consumer psychology and the increasing sophistication of the advertising industry both played a role in this change.

This once domestic-style station in Richland Center received a face-lift at some point in its history, transforming its facade to a more streamlined, modern design. Photo by Jim Draeger

A technical report by K. Lönberg-Holm in the June 1930 issue of *Architectural Record* signaled a revolutionary change in station design.[25] His study was a systematic, functional analysis of all parameters of station design including location, layout, materials and design, engineering, display, and marketing.

Lönberg-Holm made a careful study of the previous decade of station construction, revealing the most profitable locations, most effective traffic-circulation patterns, best manner of access and egress, and most efficient arrangement of fuel pumps, air hoses, stations, and service areas. He analyzed signage size, location, design, and illumination. He looked at sales data to determine the common characteristics of the most profitable locations. Lönberg-Holm even examined which colors and combinations had the highest consumer visibility. Although Lönberg-Holm did not favor any particular architectural form, his data unmistakably demonstrated the greater efficiency and profitability of the box-type station. With the rapid and almost universal adoption of this design by nearly every oil company in the early 1930s, the marketplace demonstrated its effectiveness.

A prototypical example of the box-type station. **Courtesy of Warren Baley, Steel King**

The box-type station was a simple rectangular building with a flat roof. Using concrete block or brick, builders divided it into three major zones. An operator's room stood at one corner with restrooms tucked behind. The service bays typically were located to either the right or left of the entrance. As *Architectural Forum* noted, "It is clean, unassuming, and has the inestimable virtue of looking like a filling station."[26] Stations derived their style from popular modern aesthetics such as Art Deco, Streamlined Moderne, and the International Style. Their simple, spare lines and sleek materials were in keeping with the design of the era's autos themselves and broadcast their function as gas stations in a way that the earlier domestic and civic designs failed to do.

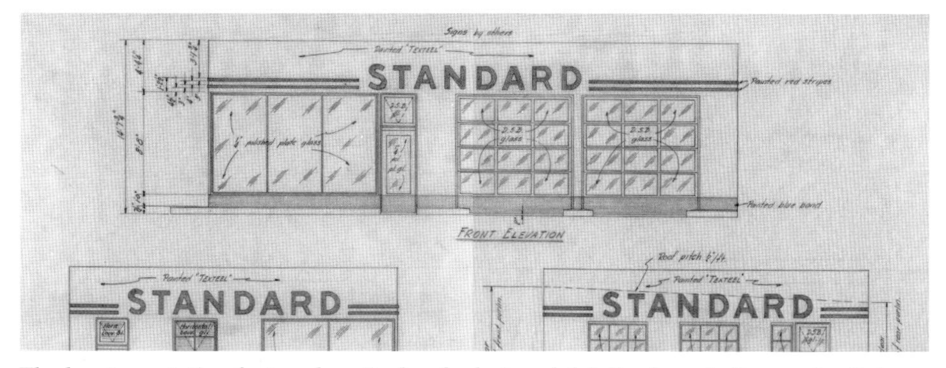

The box-type station featured meticulously designed details, down to the precise distance between stripes. **Courtesy of Warren Baley, Steel King**

Clayton Parman's station in Madison (see page 114) is a prototypical example of this new station form. Understanding the importance of prompt service, companies strove to have attendants at the pump by the time an approaching car came to a stop. The extensive plate-glass windows of the operator's room were a dramatic improvement over the tiny cottage windows of 1920s stations, creating an unobstructed view of the pump islands and driveways. From the outside, these large corner windows heightened the visibility of the sales room. Large windows also provided ample space to display the tires, batteries, and accessories (known to operators as "TBA") that were an increasing portion of station profits in the 1930s.

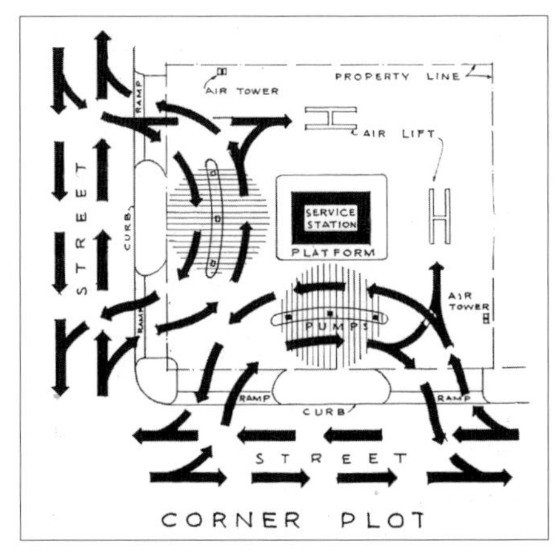

Diagrams such as this one helped station designers create efficient layouts. ***Architectural Record,* June 1930**

A corner location, such as Parman's, is the most highly desirable site for a gas station, according to Lönberg-Holm, due to its high visibility to approaching vehicles. Parman provided large parking areas as well as wide, easy approaches. Primary colors were concentrated in areas that focused attention on programmatic areas of service and sales. Garage and service bays were mostly glass and in clear sight of the pump islands. As cars passed the service bay and approached the pump island, the building functioned as its own advertisement. The box design integrated sales and service bays into a single form. Parman carefully considered lighting from a business standpoint, with the exterior lighting concentrated on the pumps and driveway rather than the building. Concrete barriers protected the pump island.

Parman's station, located on a corner lot, reflects a fundamental rethinking of gas station architecture. Photo by Jim Draeger

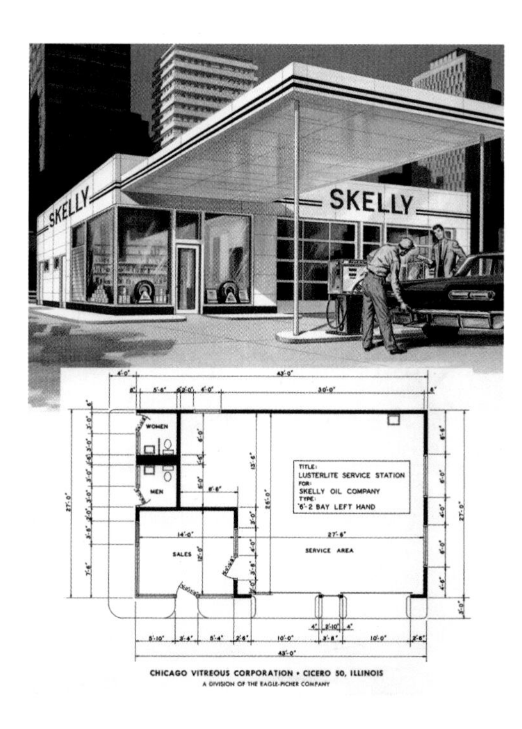

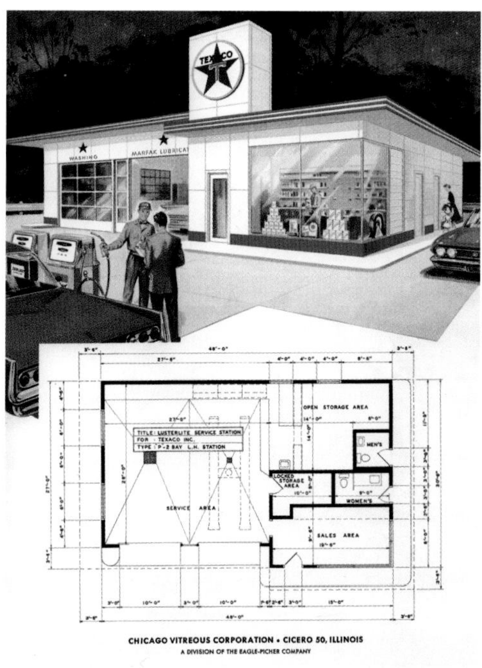

Examples of the Lusterlite Service Station, a box-type design created with variations for several companies. Chicago Vitreous Corporation

Day or night, box-type gas stations such as Parman's became three-dimensional advertisements. Functionally efficient in dispensing gasoline and providing auto service, this building form endured as long as the full-service station itself. The development and near-universal adoption by the late 1930s of a single set of design standards transformed the gas-retailing industry. The drive for efficiency even forced Pure Oil to modify its quaint cottage design in response to the dominance of the box type: a large corner window replaced the cottage window that had adorned earlier stations, as designers came to treat the operator's room as a storefront display window.

We Can Do It!
Gas Stations During the War

Nearly all oil companies, including independents, adopted standardized plans by the early 1940s, recognizing the consumers' attraction to a familiar sight in a strange place and the economic benefits of streamlining both architectural design and operations. As a result of the dominance of box-type stations, gas station buildings were increasingly engineered and constructed of steel components. Steel joists supported gas station roofs, and the buildings were clad with porcelain enamel panels and steel-framed windows. These modern materials solved many problems associated with maintenance, durability, economical cost, and ease of cleaning. In addition, manufacturers produced porcelain enamel cladding in any color scheme with patterns, logos, and other marketing devices baked into the surface. Although these technical innovations advanced the search for functional solutions in gas station design, declining sales due to wartime rationing of gasoline and rubber as well as the government's diversion of steel and other building materials into military manufacturing hampered the development of new stations.

Gas Rationing

Despite the Depression, demand for gasoline continued to grow, and more than sixty thousand new gas stations appeared between 1933 and 1940.[1] World War II had an immediate effect on American transportation and the gasoline industry. On January 5, 1942, only four weeks after the attack on Pearl Harbor, the federal government began a strict ration of rubber and tires. When a rash of gas tanker sinkings in the spring of 1942 depleted the East Coast's gasoline supplies, rationing became necessary in that region. By December 1942, however, the gas ration had been extended to the rest of the country—not because of a true gasoline shortage (except in the eastern states) but in order to control tire consumption. A coupon system provided at least some gasoline to every car, while allowing supplemental rations for occupational drivers. The government also required carpooling and strongly discouraged any unnecessary driving.[2] Although cheating and black-market activity were rampant, the system was in effect through the end of the war.[3]

Notes

1. John Margolies, *Pump and Circumstance* (Boston: Little, Brown and Company, Bullfinch Press, 1993), p. 58.
2. James Maxwell and Margaret Balcom, "Gas Rationing in the United States, I," *The Quarterly Journal of Economics* 60, no. 4 (1946): pp. 561–587; Milton Derber, "Gasoline Rationing Policy and Practice in Canada and the United States," *Journal of Marketing* 8, no. 2 (1943): pp. 137–144.
3. Margolies, p. 84.

Steel King survived the Depression through the frugal business practices of founder Walter C. Junkerman, who went so far as to draw building designs on the backs of canceled checks rather than on expensive drafting paper. World War II presented another challenge, as steel rationing forced Junkerman into a new sideline in order to keep the business afloat: manufacturing waterproof wiring harnesses and shielded cables for the army.

When America declared war on Germany in 1941, many gas attendants reported for active military duty, leaving serious staffing shortages in an industry dominated by young, service-age males. Rosie the Riveter had a gas pump counterpart as women stepped up to fill the gap. Marvel Risberg was one of the female attendants in wartime Madison. She began working the pumps

Marvel Risberg took over the pumps during World War II. WHi Image ID 34479

at her husband's Black Eagle station in 1943, when staffing became critical due to wartime labor shortages. She stayed on after the end of the war, because, as she told a *Capital Times* reporter in 1946, "My work at the station is fun."[27]

After the war ended, young families of returning veterans moved to newly built suburbs on the fringe of Wisconsin cities, and gas stations followed them. The number of stations exploded, paralleling the unprecedented suburban housing buildup associated with the baby boom. As families traveled more and commuters traveled farther, auto sales grew and demand for gasoline increased. In the new postwar suburban landscapes, the commercial strip was not inserted into an already existing streetscape but was planned, platted, and built at the same time as the neighborhoods it would serve. Gas stations defined the new suburban commercial landscape. The careful scientific planning of the Depression-era stations helped to define standards in plot size, access and egress, location preference, and other factors that postwar city planners codified in local ordinances.

Steel King hired a professional engineer in the early 1950s to oversee the increasingly complex structural demands of postwar stations. More and more, gas station construction was

Name That Slogan!

Here are advertising slogans from various oil companies. Fill in the blanks with the company name.

1. **Power to Pass... _________ Gas!**
2. **Put a Tiger in Your Tank**

   ***Extra credit:* We're Changing Our Name, but Not Our Stripes!**
3. **You Can Trust Your Car to the Man Who Wears the Star**
4. **Drive with Care and Buy _________**
5. **Gentlemen Prefer Bronze**
6. **The Performance Company**
7. **I Got Live Power**
8. **That Good _________ Gasoline**
9. **You Can Be Sure of _________**
10. **I Can Be Very Friendly**
11. **Tops in Traffic**

Northwoods Petroleum Museum, photo by Joel Heiman

Answers
1. Dixie **2.** Esso (**extra credit:** Exxon) **3.** Texaco **4.** Sinclair **5.** Conoco **6.** Phillips 66 **7.** Standard Oil **8.** Gulf **9.** Shell **10.** Sunoco **11.** Union 76

a highly specialized, technically exacting process. Steel-frame construction required structural calculations, while cost competition favored economical solutions. Specialty companies, like Steel King, streamlined gas station erection, putting up stations in a matter of weeks. Business boomed, and soon Steel King had more than two dozen crews on the road, installing more than one hundred stations a year across the Midwest for such companies as Texaco, Standard Oil, Cities Service, Sinclair, Shell, and others.

Architects and engineers advanced station design using technologically sophisticated materials, the most emblematic being porcelain enamel exterior panels. These steel panels, clad in a baked enamel finish like refrigerators and stoves of the era, were durable, low maintenance, and easy to apply.

Highway planning accelerated after the war, driven in part by national defense arguments for improved roadways. Incremental increases in federal highway funding from the mid-1940s to the mid-1950s provided the impetus for a modern highway system. Funding increased dramatically with passage of the Federal-Aid Highway Act of 1956 (popularly known as the National Interstate and Defense Highways Act of 1956). Lawmakers saw rapid

Interstate Grand Opening

Miss Concrete and Miss Black Top preside over the grand opening of Wisconsin's first interstate highway, 1958.
WHi Image ID 1873

Miss Concrete and Miss Black Top shared the scissors with Governor Vernon Thomson to cut the ribbon at Goerke's Corners in Waukesha County, inaugurating Wisconsin's first seven-mile stretch of interstate highway on September 4, 1958.[1]

Although the nationwide system of interstate highways was a post–World War II phenomenon, its roots go back much earlier. In 1919, it took a young Dwight Eisenhower two months to travel from Washington, D.C., to San Francisco in a military convoy that averaged only six miles an hour. This experience—as well as the sight of the German autobahn during World War II—helped make road development one of Eisenhower's priorities when he became president in 1953. America had toyed with highway-improvement plans in the 1920s and 1930s; serious planning began after World War II. Eisenhower signed the Federal-Aid Highway Act of 1956, providing federal funds to construct the forty-one-thousand-mile "National System of Interstate and Defense Highways."

Notes

1. Wisconsin Department of Transportation, "Transportation History, Interstate 50th Anniversary: 50 Interstate Facts," www.dot.wisconsin.gov/library/history/50/facts.htm.

deployment of military forces using the interstate system as a vital component of military readiness. The act coincided with groundbreaking for Wisconsin's first limited-access freeway (I-94) near Goerke's Corners. Interstate highways changed the nature of gas retailing, clustering stations near entrance and exit ramps. Land-acquisition costs rose dramatically for these choice sites, while existing stations found themselves located along the back roads or orphaned along former highways that became frontage roads of business routes to the interstates that replaced them.

Interstate highways reorganized many communities' commercial landscapes, leaving once-busy streets empty and causing businesses to move closer to highway interchanges and off-ramps. Collection of Mark Speltz

Keep on Lickin'

One of the most popular and enduring promotions used by American gas stations was the S&H Green Stamp program. S&H (Sperry and Hutchinson) Green Stamps were first issued in 1896, and the promotion reached its peak in the late 1960s. Gas stations and other businesses purchased the stamps from S&H and doled them out a few stamps at a time to customers to encourage customer loyalty and repeat business. Green Stamp recipients pasted the stamps into special books they could redeem through the mail or at S&H stores. While most consumers opted for ordinary prizes—cutlery, toasters, televisions—S&H was apparently willing to accommodate more outlandish requests, including a Pennsylvania school's 5.4 million stamp collection, which they exchanged for a pair of gorillas for their local zoo![1]

The Green Stamp program slowed in the 1970s. The economy was in a slump, and as profit margins slimmed, gas stations dispensed with free giveaways such as drinking glasses, matchbooks, road maps, and the once-popular Green Stamps. At one time, nearly every retailer handed out stamps, which diminished the loyalty incentive that retailers desired.[2] Today, however, you can still redeem old Green Stamps from the attic—and the concept has found a new life online as "greenpoints" earned through Internet purchases.[3]

Notes

1. "Whatever Happened to Green Stamps?" *The Straight Dope Staff Report,* www.straightdope.com.
2. Mary Pollack, "Green Stamps: A Case Study," *Journal of Services Marketing* 2, no. 4 (Fall 1988): pp. 37–40.
3. S&H Greenpoints, www.greenpoints.com.

WHi Image ID 56236

This Wisconsin Dells Sinclair station prominently advertised its clean restrooms. WHi Image ID 42214

Between 1956 and 1969, when Wisconsin constructed its initial interstate system, oil companies speculated on station construction along these new corridors. Ralph Maas anticipated that a planned expressway interchange in Glendale would provide a profitable location for a new Phillips 66 station. When the interchange was never constructed, this unsuccessful gamble left the station stranded along Port Washington Road competing with eleven other stations for local road traffic. The interstate proved a boom for some and a bust for others as massive transportation shifts occurred.

In the postwar marketplace, competition for gasoline sales was increasingly national. The largest oil companies, such as Shell and Texaco, expanded their reach and stepped up their marketing campaigns, looking for a bigger share. The market saturation that followed this station-construction boom resulted in tweaking of the then ubiquitous box-type stations. Maas's Glendale station (see page 96) was an example of the Phillips 66 contribution to this fresh, new, modern postwar aesthetic: company architect Clarence Reinhardt added a soaring bat-wing canopy and canted windows to the basic box, mirroring the sharp lines seen elsewhere in automobile culture.

New publicity campaigns once again emphasized service and clean restrooms, unleashing the "white glove" brigades that traveled coast to coast enforcing cleanliness standards on individual stations and creating a media blitz. As a result, the men's restroom lost its place in the man-space of the operator's room. It was relocated to the station's side, adjacent to the ladies' restroom; male patrons no longer shared the oil- and grease-soaked sinks with mechanics and operators. The gender inequalities of early-twentieth-century station designs receded—foreshadowing, perhaps, the emergence of the women's rights movement. Designers no longer treated women as special in the spatial design of the station, and men gained restrooms cleaned to the same standard as women's restrooms.

Icing the Box Cake

Stations Get a Makeover

By the late 1950s and early 1960s, the highway-beautification movement took root as, once again, opposition grew to the visual clutter along the roadside. The issue gathered steam as Lady Bird Johnson took up the cause, convening a White House summit on improving gas station design. The flashy, flamboyant buildings of the postwar era were considered unsightly icons to those who campaigned for aesthetic controls along the roadside.

Growing public concern for the environment also caused changes in the appearance and operation of gas stations. Lead additives in gasoline formulations, used to prevent engine knocking caused by improper fuel combustion, had been around since the 1920s. In the mid-1960s, Clair Patterson, a geochemist, refuted the widely held belief, supported by the oil industry, that small concentrations of lead in the bloodstream were relatively harmless. Patterson further demonstrated that growing lead levels in the environment correlated with increasing numbers of automobiles. Leaded gasoline became the prime suspect. Growing concern for clean air and water, led by grassroots advocates, resulted in the passage of the first Clean Air Act in 1963, which in part mandated stricter emissions controls for cars. Congress gradually phased out leaded gas, but the oil and auto industries both became targets of the emerging environmental movement.

Knock-Knock

One annoyance common to early cars was "engine knock," a pinging noise made by overworked engines. The problem—premature gasoline ignition—was caused by low-octane fuel. In 1921, General Motors engineers Thomas Midgeley, Thomas Boyd, and Charles Ketterling discovered that knocking could be alleviated by adding lead tetraethyl—TEL—to gasoline. And ethyl gas was born.[1]

Although lead was a known poison—*Scientific American* referred to it as such as early as 1857[2]—TEL was needed only in tiny quantities, causing scientists and public health officials to believe that the small amounts would not be damaging.[3]

Advances in engine design and improved refining techniques gradually lessened the knocking problem. The United States phased out leaded gasoline in the 1970s and 1980s, amid growing awareness about the hazards of lead poisoning and the environmental degradation caused by even low levels of the dangerous metal.

Notes

1. Jack Lewis, "Lead Poisoning: A Historical Perspective," *EPA Journal*, May 1985.
2. Septimus Piesse, "Sugar of Lead," *Scientific American*, August 29, 1857, p. 403.
3. William Kovarik, Ph.D., "Ethyl: The 1920s Environmental Conflict Over Leaded Gasoline and Alternative Fuels" (paper to the American Society for Environmental History, Annual Conference, Providence, RI, March 26–30, 2003).

This Steel King plan shows the conversion of an existing box-type station into a mansard look. **Courtesy of Warren Baley, Steel King**

Oil companies were initially slow to respond to the environmental and beautification movements. Although they were reluctant to deviate from the clean, modern, efficient marketing image expressed by box-type stations, increased zoning restrictions forced them to alter their station designs. Communities threatened oil companies with construction moratoriums, voluntary reduction of the number of stations allowed for each chain, exclusion from certain types of commercial zoning, and design review to force their cooperation in making stations more aesthetically pleasing. The archetypal image of the modern box-type full-service station that gas retailers had painstakingly crafted over the course of three decades of marketing was changed not by business practices but by social forces.

The architectural makeover was twofold. Large oil chains, saddled with ragtag collections of stations spanning decades, looked for a quick and cost-effective solution. Owners covered existing box-type stations in a thin skin of brick veneer, stucco, or vertical board-and-batten "barn board." Critics viewed this return to traditional, more natural building materials instead of the sleek, machined appearance of porcelain enamel exteriors as a concession toward

The suburban ranch station's more "naturalistic" design—with brick- or stonework and details borrowed from the California ranch house. **Courtesy of O. J. Thompto**

sensitive design. False, shingle-clad mansard roofs, which topped most station makeovers, became an aesthetic cliché of the late 1960s and early 1970s. Weathered shingles attempted to evoke an appearance consistent with the natural wood aesthetic that came to characterize residential design in this period.

New stations received more extensive changes. Taking a cue from the residential station types of the 1920s, companies offered a similar solution to the same problem of fitting in. Companies again modeled their stations after domestic architecture. In this case, ranch-style post-and-beam roofs, brick chimneys, and soft colors disguised the nearly unchanged space planning of the box-type station. These new domestic-looking stations created a brilliantly conceived aesthetic that critics could not challenge without assailing the housing tastes of a generation of postwar suburbanites.

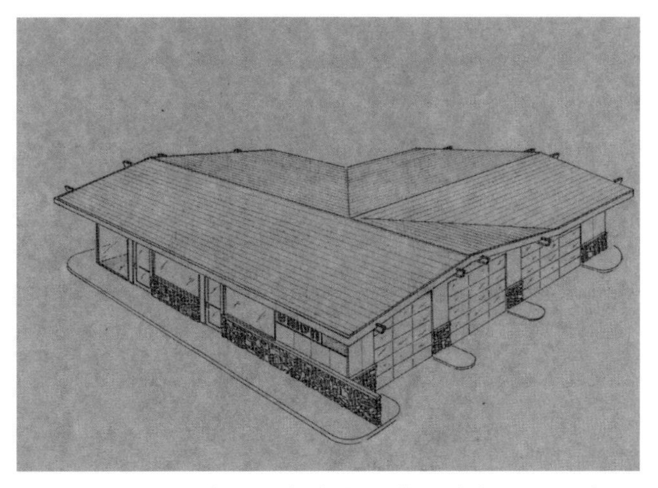

The variation on the ranch design allowed for service bays.
Courtesy of Warren Baley, Steel King

Don't You Call It a Gas Station?

Self-Service and the Convenience Store

The final gasp of the full-service station began during the oil embargo of 1973, when reduced production by OPEC (Organization of Petroleum Exporting Countries) members caused prices to skyrocket by 40 percent over a few months.[28] Greater fuel efficiency stemming from both an increase in smaller, imported cars and federal gas mileage standards adopted in 1975 coupled with decreased recreational driving caused a marked drop in fuel consumption. Caught flat-footed by the decreased demand, major oil companies shuttered full-service stations by the thousands, unable to compete in the changing marketplace as high-volume, multipump independents such as Wisconsin's Clark Oil Company rewrote the book with their lean, efficient operations. By 1970, Clark operated 1,489 stations and refined almost 100,000 barrels of crude oil a day.

Emory T. Clark's premium-only strategy produced a higher-than-average profit margin, insulating his company from the price wars that consumed the industry. His emphasis on high-traffic locations allowed the company to sell almost twice the national average of gallons per location. By the 1970s, his Milwaukee-based operation had become the most successful independent oil marketer and refiner in the Midwest. But the market changes following the OPEC embargo would soon force Clark to change his business model.

This Brookfield station along a well-traversed road in 1962 was one where Emory T. Clark relied on his premium-only strategy. WHi Image ID 40878

While self-serve stations had been around since California independent George Ulrich opened his first in 1946, they became the norm in the 1970s as slim profits resulting from downward price pressures were further reduced by competition from cost-cutting independents. Gas stations were making less per gallon of gasoline while labor costs remained steady, causing service stations to also go self-serve as a means of controlling expenses. This transition to self-service gas pumps revolutionized the industry, overturning a service model as old as the gas station itself. The rapid pace of change was likewise dramatic. About 1 percent of the gas market was self-service in 1969; six years later it topped 35 percent, and within a little more than a decade it climbed to nearly 75 percent of all sales.[29]

Despite the fact that women had worked in mom-and-pop operations from the early days of filling stations and kept stations running during wartime labor shortages, for most of the history of full-service, the pump island was a male space. With the transition to self-service, the gas station once again became a reflection of gender issues: a woman pumping her own gas challenged the cultural stereotype of the helpless female motorist. A vestige of masculine

The social and economic changes of the 1970s saw women embracing self-service at the gas station. Courtesy of O. J. Thompto

domination disappeared, and stations became reflective of the struggle for gender equality.

The consumer became a pump jockey, and service station design evolved once again as the pump island canopy returned. Largely abandoned by the 1930s due to the high costs of construction, the canopy came back as a freestanding structure and an essential marketing feature of new self-service stations. Although canopies were still costly, once the customer became a pump operator, it made business sense to shelter self-service pumps from sun, rain, sleet, and snow. Longtime gas station manufacturer Steel King transitioned from station fabrication to the highly specialized gas station canopy market. The engineering demands of these new canopies to withstand snow loads, high winds, and accidental damage created a niche for Steel King, which became one of about a dozen firms nationwide to construct this new symbol of the self-service revolution.

The emergence of the combination convenience store and gas station also threatened the full-service station. By the late 1970s, cut-rate price competition from convenience stores, discounters, and high-volume pumpers squeezed profit margins to a few cents per gallon. By

Why I Collect

"**[When I discover hidden memorabilia in an attic, it]** isn't necessarily the object that I liked, it was ...being with the person who had used these things, had owned these things. Finding these things that hadn't been looked at in years, and making an offer. I can remember I think I offered him a hundred dollars, [and] I got all the [gas pump] globes, I got signs—all kinds of things. And I remember driving back and forth to Hollandale with my little car hauling all of that stuff. So it isn't any one particular object. It's the experience that you have in looking for it and finding it. It's a little bit like I suppose an archaeologist who's out there digging. You know, he doesn't know what he's digging for and all of a sudden he finds something. And you know it's a great experience. That's kind of like I call myself an archaeologist in a way because I like finding something that's kind of hidden, buried and so forth." —*O. J. Thompto, gas station memorabilia collector, Madison*[1]

Notes

1. O. J. Thompto, interview by David Hestad, Wisconsin Public Television, September 20, 2006.

With the advent of self-service, the canopy returned. Courtesy of Warren Baley, Steel King

the 1980s, many older stations were having financial trouble and began to sell groceries and other convenience items. Auto-service bays became aisles stocked with beverages and food, and the distinction between convenience store and gas station disappeared. From that point forward, the large chains began designing new self-serve units with convenience stores. Industry organ *National Petroleum News* reported in 1984 that "Nobody is building your conventional three-bay service station any longer."[30]

The number of gas stations shrunk precipitously as competition squeezed out less-profitable stations. The change surprised Necedah full-service station owner Clarence Jaeger. He repeated this conversation to *Milwaukee Journal Sentinel* reporter Dennis McCann:

> I had a woman in here awhile back from Schaumburg [Ill.]. She said she ran a Mobil Store there. I said, "What's a Mobil Store?" She said, "You know, like you have, only with a store."
>
> I said, "Don't you call it a gas station?"[31]

These market changes are reflected in the operations of the Clark chain. By the late 1970s, higher crude oil costs increased wholesale gas prices, which combined with thinner profit margins to squeeze Clark's profits. New CEO Robert G. Reed III restructured operations, closing almost four hundred unprofitable locations, building new high-volume "superstations," and converting most stations to self-service. The company hired a former executive of the 7-11 and Stop-N-Go convenience store chains to convert existing Clark stations to convenience store operations. By 1981, the Clark family sold the company to Apex Oil, an indication of larger, nationwide consolidations resulting from the turmoil of late-twentieth-century operations.

The era of full-service stations was rapidly coming to an end. High-tech vehicles with electronic ignitions and computer-controlled engines squeezed out stations offering auto repair as a sideline, as owners of these stations were unable to afford expensive electronic diagnostics and the costs of training employees to use these new technologies. By the 1990s, fewer than half of all gas stations offered auto-repair services; they'd lost ground to the newly emerging specialty auto-repair shops offering tires, rapid oil changes, brakes, mufflers, and many of the simple repairs that had been the mainstay of the full-service station.

The cascading effect of price wars, competition from self-service stations, convenience store additions, and competition from specialty repair shops destroyed the financial model of the full-service gas station, ushering in an era of dramatic change.

I've Got LUST!

Leaking Tanks in the Environmental Era

In the late twentieth century, the number of shuttered and abandoned station sites revealed the extent of an issue that had lurked for decades. Underground tanks, which had transformed early gas retailing by allowing gasoline to be safely stored belowground, had now become an environmental hazard. Leaking underground storage tanks (known to regulators as LUSTs) contaminated soil and threatened drinking water. Plumes of petroleum traveled unseen below the surface only to be discovered as old station sites were purchased for redevelopment.

By 1988, federal and state environmental laws placed stringent controls on underground tanks, requiring leak detection, inspection, corrosion protection, overflow controls, and tank removal at closed sites. Many independent station owners could not afford the significant cost of remediation or increased liability insurance. In October 1998, when the deadline for upgrading its tanks approached, Parman's Super Service Station pulled its tanks. Unable to address these environmental concerns, many other owners of smaller stations pulled their pumps or abandoned their stations. The era of the full-service station came to a lurching end.

Abandoned station sites became black eyes for oil companies as the carefully crafted architectural forms that they had intentionally incorporated into their market image were boarded up. Some embarked upon systematic demolition of old stations; others marketed those sites for rehabilitation or adaptive reuse.

As troublesome as old station sites could be, entrepreneurs appreciated the prime locations occupied by old stations and, beginning in the 1980s, began to adapt those stations to clever new uses that traded on gas station imagery. Madison developer Joe Krupp converted Severson's Service Station into a popular diner called Monty's Blue Plate (see page 116), and Michael's Frozen Custard built a Madison chain of restaurants in old gas stations. But perhaps the most successful adaptive reuse is the gas-to-riches story of Sherman Perk in Milwaukee (see page 124).

The last quarter of the twentieth century saw many station owners get out of the business, leaving behind ugly, deserted buildings such as this one in Wauwatosa. WHi Image ID 57270

The Streamlined Moderne Copeland Service Station, completed in 1939 by the flamboyantly monikered

Milwaukee architect Urban F. Peacock, pumped its last gas in 1990. A subsequent owner left the building, sitting on a contaminated site, in tax delinquency. The low point came when the station became Milwaukee's poster child for condemnation, pictured in an article entitled "Rid Your Neighborhood of Eyesores: City Can Help by Condemning Buildings."[32] But a vigorous preservation campaign by the Sherman Park neighborhood culminated in the station's designation as a Milwaukee landmark and its architecturally sensitive rebirth as Sherman Perk, a coffee shop cleverly named to honor the neighborhood that rallied to save it. Then-mayor John Norquist closed the circle of renewal, presenting the new owners, Bob and Patrice Olin, with the Mayor's Design Award in 2001.

Running on Empty
The End of an Era

Most historic stations have vanished from the built landscape of the twenty-first century, but the age of gas station nostalgia has dawned, bringing hope to the legions of avid historic preservationists, roadside scholars, vintage car collectors, and petroliana collectors who see meaning in the ordinary stations of the past. Just as railroad buffs saved scores of historic depots in the late 1900s, advocates of gas stations are converting stations to inventive new uses that celebrate their former glory. The growing number of gas station books—from collectors' guides to pumps, oilcans, and other petroliana to photo essays of vanished stations and scholarly works like *The Gas Station in America*—indicate that Americans increasingly regard gas stations as important artifacts of the twentieth century.

Rid Your Neighborhood of Eyesores:
City can help by condemning buildings

Not all old buildings are well-preserved examples of our rich architectural heritage. Some old buildings are just plain eyesores.

Of the 255,000 dwelling units in Milwaukee, more than 74 percent of them were built prior to 1950. Every year, a number of these buildings -- ranging from garages to commercial structures -- are demolished by the city because they have become heavily damaged by fire and vandalism, or have become so deteriorated that they are a neighborhood blight.

But the city must follow a well-established and complex set of procedures before demolishing a building.

The building tagged for demolition first is inspected by a certified city inspector, generally stemming from a complaint or a referral from a neighbor. The inspector must determine if the cost of repairs would exceed half the assessed valuation of the building.

If the inspector determines that demolition is called for, a title search is ordered to find the true owner. Once found, the property owner is personally served with a demolition notice. The owner then has 30 days to either demolish the building or seek a court order preventing it.

Property owners are required to show either a plan for rehabilitating the building, or else show that the building is not as deteriorated as the city's original report shows.

If demolition still is ordered, the city solicits bids from demolition contractors. The average cost of this demolition is about $7,500. The city then requires property owners to reimburse these costs.

Once the contract is signed, the contractor has 30-90 days to demolish the building, grade over the site and add topsoil and grass seed.

City officials admit that the various steps added to insure that no one's property is taken without due process can slow the procedure down. But they stress that the process is thorough, and that the entire demolition process can turn what once was a neighborhood eyesore into an asset.

Ald. George Butler (right) and neighborhood activists Larry Garland and Kathleen Jackson want the owners of this abandoned service station at 4924 W. Roosevelt Dr. to demolish the eyesore and clean up the deteriorated property.

Children Do Better with a Healthy Start

Health care reform may be a highlight of the new administration, but for many, the wait may be too costly. If you need help paying for the health care you and your children need, Wisconsin's Healthy Start program may be able to help.

Healthy Start pays for medical care for pregnant women, babies and young children. Even families with health care insurance may apply. Children ages 6 and older may be eligible, but must meet lower income level guidelines. Most babies are covered up until they are one year old, even if the family's income goes up.

Healthy Start pays for all doctor visits and hospital costs, prescription drugs, delivery of a baby, health care (medical, dental and vision care) for pregnant women, up until 60 days following delivery, and health care for children born after September 30, 1983.

To learn where applications are available, call **286-2533**. Or, to have an application mailed to you, call the Healthy Start Outreach Coordinator at **286-8830**.

The former Copeland Service Station in Milwaukee was the poster child for ugly abandoned buildings before it was renovated into the Sherman Perk coffee shop. Courtesy of Cliff Leppke, personal papers

Nostalgia for full-service stations is strong in the generations that grew up with them. Robert Broetzman's personal nostalgia for the 1940s, when he hand-cranked gas at the visible pumps of his father's station, led him to rescue the Town of Maple Valley filling station (see page 154) to serve as a backdrop for his growing collection of pumps, signs, and accessories. The rescue and purchase of Frank Seneca's station—a pagoda-style Wadhams station that has become a treasured landmark—by the City of West Allis and its restoration as a local museum is a civic commitment to automobile history (see page 142). Stories like these are being repeated in Wisconsin communities such as DePere, Brooklyn, and Independence as we awaken to the realization that if we don't act soon, these humble buildings will vanish and their stories will be lost.

Removing the gasoline tanks at the Copeland Service Station in Milwaukee, part of its rehabilitation into Sherman Perk. Courtesy of Bob Olin

It is hard to imagine that similar nostalgia will compel us to someday preserve the bland, boxy convenience stores that have replaced full-service stations. Unlike the friendly personal service of the past, modern gas dispensing is an anonymous act, which, thanks to pay-at-the-pump, no longer even requires a face-to-face transaction. Gas retailing has become impersonal. Like the neighborhood tavern, the corner grocery, and the local hardware store, the neighborhood gas station has fallen victim to larger, more efficient, cost-cutting operations, physically removed from us and only tangentially connected to our lives. Although many of us value the speed and convenience of new stations, the rich social dimension that marked gas stations of the past has been lost.

Gas stations have mirrored changes in the broader culture that gave rise to them. From the crude shacks of the early twentieth century onward, stations changed as the social, economic, and political forces that created them evolved over time. Gas stations played a pivotal role in our auto age. Their builders pioneered auto-related community planning, giving birth to the commercial strip and creating prototypes for nearly all detached "drive-in" structures. Gas companies were at the forefront of the development of twentieth-century corporate image through the use of consumer psychology and marketing. The surviving stations of each era are three-dimensional slices of our past, objects that

Food not gas is now the fuel of choice at Monty's Blue Plate Diner in Madison. This former station once again serves as a lively neighborhood meeting place. WHS Accession 2008/088, photo by Joel Heiman

In Memoriam

As we researched and wrote *Fill 'er Up*, several notable examples of historic gas station architecture fell by the wayside—literally: either demolished or so drastically altered as to prevent their inclusion. Our hope is that this book engenders a sense of stewardship of these places that tell us much about where we've been and how we've gotten to where we are today.

One that we were most saddened to lose was the log cabin-style station in the Town of Cassian (we kept this entry, see page 148, as a sort of call to action in the name of historic preservation). We also miss the small Standard Oil station in Stoughton; the Van Beek station in Allenton; the Harley Sprague Wadhams station in Milwaukee; and the Badger Country station in Antigo.

Demolished Stoughton Standard Oil station. Photo by Jim Draeger

A number of stations were so questionably modified since we had seen them years ago that we decided to not include them: the station in Eau Claire that had received a National Register of Historic Places designation; the tiled-roof Greek Revival station in rural Fond du Lac County (which was horribly altered); a Hazel Green station that is today somewhat of a museum/repair garage; and the Richland Center station on page 36 (its porcelain enamel panels were gone when we last saw it).

Fond du Lac County station, prior to a recent update. Photo by James A. Sewell

Rehabilitation tax credits and brownfield grants have helped fund preservation efforts at stations in Cedarburg, Kenosha, and Milwaukee. We hope other station owners, communities, and local preservationists will seek out information on these programs to save—and perhaps transform via an adaptive reuse as a twenty-first-century neighborhood meeting spot—their examples of Wisconsin roadside architecture. Some information about federal tax credits is available at www.nps.gov/history/tax.htm.

Robert Broetzman is one of the many petroliana enthusiasts who share our sentiments. His Rust in Peace cemetery in the Town of Maple Valley is his homage to the glory days of Wisconsin gas stations.

Robert Broetzman's tribute to the history of gas. WHS Accession 2008/088, photo by Mark Fay

tell the stories of time and place. As times changed, so, too, did gas stations. The evolving marketplace and intense competition have left us with only handfuls of historic gas stations to express this complex and rich history.

As we begin the twenty-first century, it appears clear that while gas stations continue to vanish, automobiles show no signs of decline. Alternative fuels, such as hydrogen, ethanol, and biodiesel, and new hybrid, fuel cell, or electric vehicles may one day come to displace gasoline-powered internal combustion engines. Any of these will likely give rise to new building types that will evolve to become more efficient and mirror historical, cultural, and environmental forces. A sign of change might be the PrairieFire BioFuels Cooperative, a biodiesel station located, not surprisingly, in an old gas station on East Washington Avenue in Madison.

The future is uncertain, but the past is clear. We invite you to hit the road and explore the gas stations presented in this book, or those remaining in your communities, and reflect upon the historical patterns of change that created them.

WISCONSIN

•

SINCLAIR

Road Map

SINCLAIR

FOR A ROUTE
TO THE
WORLD'S FAIR
WRITE SINCLAIR

SINCLAIR

Collection of Mark Speltz

59 Historic Stations

Your Guide to Hitting the Road

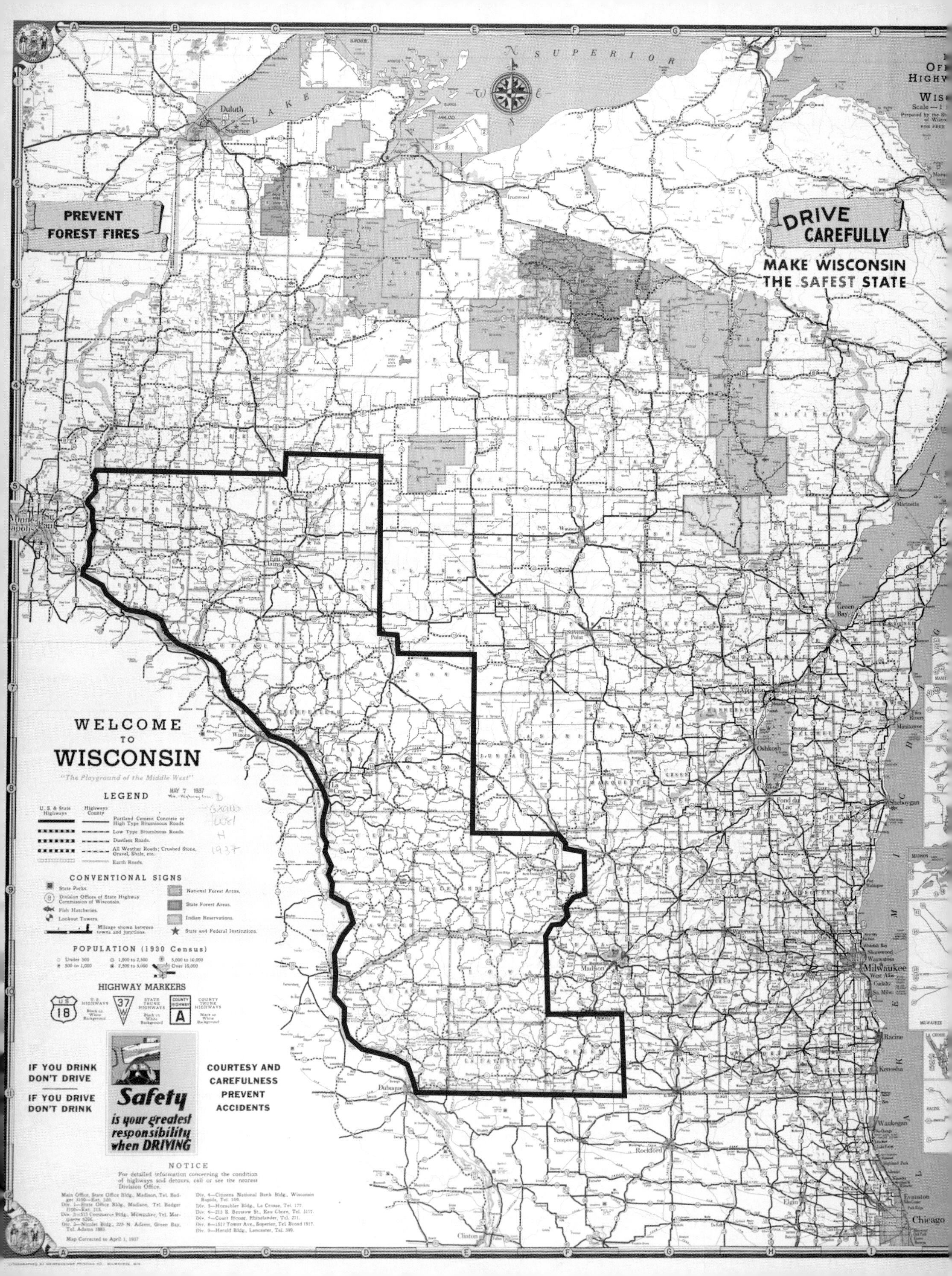

LAKE SUPERIOR
Duluth
Superior
Ironwood
PREVENT FOREST FIRES
DRIVE CAREFULLY
MAKE WISCONSIN THE SAFEST STATE
Minneapolis
St. Paul
Eau Claire
Wausau
Marinette
Green Bay
Stevens Point
Appleton
Oshkosh
Two Rivers
Manitowoc
Winona
La Crosse
Fond du Lac
Sheboygan
Madison
Milwaukee
West Allis
Racine
Kenosha
Janesville
Beloit
Dubuque
Freeport
Rockford
Waukegan
Evanston
Chicago
Clinton
WELCOME TO WISCONSIN
"The Playground of the Middle West"
MAY 7 1937
LEGEND
U. S. & State Highways
Highways County
Portland Cement Concrete or High Type Bituminous Roads.
Low Type Bituminous Roads.
Dustless Roads.
All Weather Roads; Crushed Stone, Gravel, Shale, etc.
Earth Roads.
CONVENTIONAL SIGNS
State Parks.
Division Offices of State Highway Commission of Wisconsin.
Fish Hatcheries.
Lookout Towers.
Mileage shown between towns and junctions.
National Forest Areas.
State Forest Areas.
Indian Reservations.
State and Federal Institutions.
POPULATION (1930 Census)
Under 500
500 to 1,000
1,000 to 2,500
2,500 to 5,000
5,000 to 10,000
Over 10,000
HIGHWAY MARKERS
US 18
U. S. HIGHWAYS Black on White Background
37 W
STATE TRUNK HIGHWAYS Black on White Background
COUNTY HIGHWAY A
COUNTY TRUNK HIGHWAYS Black on White Background
IF YOU DRINK DON'T DRIVE
IF YOU DRIVE DON'T DRINK
Safety is your greatest responsibility when DRIVING
COURTESY AND CAREFULNESS PREVENT ACCIDENTS
NOTICE
For detailed information concerning the condition of highways and detours, call or see the nearest Division Office.
Main Office, State Office Bldg., Madison, Tel. Badger 3100—Ext. 320.
Div. 1—State Office Bldg., Madison, Tel. Badger 3100—Ext. 315.
Div. 2—513 Commerce Bldg., Milwaukee, Tel. Marquette 6396.
Div. 3—Nicolet Bldg., 225 N. Adams, Green Bay, Tel. Adams 1883.
Div. 4—Citizens National Bank Bldg., Wisconsin Rapids, Tel. 109.
Div. 5—Hoeschler Bldg., La Crosse, Tel. 177.
Div. 6—213 S. Barstow St., Eau Claire, Tel. 3177.
Div. 7—Court House, Rhinelander, Tel. 271.
Div. 8—1517 Tower Ave., Superior, Tel. Broad 1917.
Div. 9—Herald Bldg., Lancaster, Tel. 399.
Map Corrected to April 1, 1937

WEST

1. Cochrane
2. Darlington
3. El Paso
4. Independence
5. La Crosse
6. Mineral Point
7. Monroe
8. Platteville
9. Prairie du Sac
10. Rockbridge
11. South Lancaster
12. Spring Green
13. Stoddard

Cochrane

402 South Main Street

When Henry E. Kochenderfer opened this service station in 1933, he threw quite a grand party to dedicate it. He and his family served free beer and food; there was even a free dance that night, though not at the station but at the village's pavilion. The local newspaper invited everyone to visit and inspect what they described as a new sign of progress. The station clearly had symbolic importance for a small community like Cochrane.

Outlined in blue and white neon with the Kochenderfer name along the peak, the station's steeply pitched roof beckoned to nighttime travelers on nearby State Highway 35. Locally produced tile and brick were used along the building's base and in the gables, and a clock was set in the front gable over the entrance. The large structure featured an enclosed service bay for oiling and greasing automobiles, an office, and separate wash and restrooms for men and women. The three pumps out front proudly dispensed Phillips 66 gasoline, the only brand that would ever be sold at the station.

Although the building was emblazoned with the Kochenderfer name, Henry actually built the station for his daughter Pearl and son-in-law George Staak. They lived in the residential space behind the office and on the second floor, an uncommon but practical feature in service-station design for owners or operators who worked long hours. The Staaks ran the station and lived there the entire fifty-six years it was in use. After George died in 1978, Pearl continued to sell gasoline—and, more important to local schoolchildren, candy—until the pumps were removed in 1989.

The Kochenderfer family outside their service station, ca. 1933.
Courtesy of Marian Engfer

Courtesy of Marian Engfer

WHS Accession 2008/088, photo by Mark Fay

Gas pump globe.
Northwoods Petroleum Museum, photo by Joel Heiman

2 Darlington

404 Main Street

When the Iowa Oil Company built this station along Darlington's Main Street, the local paper bragged that it gave the "impression of a temple or a college chapel, and not just another oil station."[1]

Inspired by technological and industrial advances, the owners chose the Art Moderne style for their impressive station, constructed in 1931. The super-service station, built with grime-resistant, white glazed brick, was adorned with a jet-black brick beltcourse (a horizontal band of bricks) and a pair of two-story polygonal towers topped with green signage. In addition to three white gas pumps out front, a large multisided glass display case sat near the sidewalk and was lit up at night. Wisely, the case was elevated on a sizable concrete base to protect it from erratic drivers.

The station operators invited motorists to take advantage of their wide range of services and products, from Cities Service Oils and Koolmotor gasoline to Firestone Tires and Willard Batteries. While many service stations had only one or two service bays, this one featured four. The mechanics in the roomy repair area were set up to handle brakes, lubrication, tires, and car washing among other tasks. Motorists could have everything on their automobile taken care of at one convenient location.

The original operators of the station were Art Richter and R. E. "Earl" McConnell. After a few interim changes in management, Henry Meyers took over the lease in 1959; his son, Gene, purchased the station in 1976. Gas stopped flowing from the pumps in 1988. The spacious structure continued to operate as a repair garage into the new millennium, before going up for sale in 2007.

Gas pump globe.
Northwoods Petroleum Museum, photo by Joel Heiman

Northwoods Petroleum Museum, photo by Joel Heiman

WHS Accession 2008/088, photo by Mark Fay

3 El Paso

W4212 County Road 6

The logs of this small station have quite a long history. An El Paso pioneer, Knute Bjornson, built a log house in the 1860s that later was damaged in a 1930 tornado. In 1933, Knute's enterprising grandson, Cooney Bjornson, dismantled and reassembled the humble log building to house a gas station and tavern business.

Cooney installed a single gasoline pump in front of the structure and leased it to G. Lewis Bowen. In May 1937, Ernie Seifert bought the business from Cooney. Seifert, who did a little mechanical work at the Log Cabin Bar, had experience patching and vulcanizing tubes. He began changing oil in an outdoor pit, but that was discontinued due to safety concerns. Seifert kept busy with tire work during the years of World War II when rubber was rationed and new tires were hard to get.

Seifert's family helped keep the bar and gas sales going into at least the 1970s. Removal of the underground tanks in the mid-1980s sealed the gas station's final days as a commercial venture.

Adolph Johnson purchased the log cabin bar and nearby house in 1992 and treats it more like a personal cabin than a business. If Johnson's there sipping a beer with a friend and passersby stop in, they're welcomed. The old log cabin is guaranteed to be open and overflowing with customers one weekend in August during the annual El Paso Days.

WHS Accession 2008/088, photo by Mark Fay

Independence

23923 Burrows Road

Curious current-day travelers motoring through Independence often are tempted to pull into this former Texaco service station. A pair of vintage pumps complete with Texaco globes and a fanfare of period signage beckon from a station that looks nearly identical to its original state. The only things missing are the gasoline and an attendant ready to dash out the door to offer full-service.

Owner Loren Nelson operates an auto-repair business in the former Texaco station. Following an aneurysm, Nelson decided to follow his true passion: he restored the station, outfitting it with historically accurate petroliana.

Leo Breska built the station in 1931 as State Highway 93 (now Burrows Road) was being improved. Better roads meant more traffic, and soon there were five stations selling gasoline in the small community.

Breska leased his station to Texaco for one half of a cent per gallon of gas sold. He constructed his new station with hollow, fireproof tiles and clad it with stucco for a southwestern feel (evoking the indigenous architecture of America's richest oil-producing region) that reinforced Texaco's market image. Rounded arch doors and front windows decorated the uniquely styled structure. When the single service bay on the back of the building proved insufficient, two additional bays with multi-pane doors were added.

Nelson loves working in this distinctive setting more than seventy-five years after it opened. His affection for this jewel of a station is shared by scores of nostalgic travelers who can't resist stopping at the pumps for an authentic glimpse of gas retailing's golden age.

Breska's station before its service bay additions.
Courtesy of Loren Nelson

WHS Accession 2008/088, photo by Mark Fay

WHS Accession 2008/088, photo by Mark Fay

5 La Crosse

400 Cass Street

This charming English Cottage-style Pure Oil service station sprawls over much of the corner lot of Cass and South Fourth streets in La Crosse.

A gas station was first constructed on this corner in 1928; a few years later it became a Pure Oil station. In 1937, when Henry Ott reopened the station, it was billed as the city's newest "shopping center" for motorists and promised "Flowers to the ladies, Cigars for the men, and suckers for the kiddies" at the formal opening.[2]

The station had been remodeled to reflect the Pure Oil Company's standardized quaint and homey design that Carl A. Petersen, a Pure Oil architect, had developed as part of the company's corporate identity. The company placed its bright blue and white corporate colors on oilcans, gas pumps, and signage as well as on the steeply pitched "Pure Oil blue" tile roof featured at stations such as this one. Motorists knew that if it had a blue roof, it was a Pure Oil station. By 1938, the Pure Oil Company was selling its products in almost seventeen thousand branded outlets.

In addition to the iconic roof, tall chimneys on the ends of the building were another visible centerpiece of Pure Oil's English Cottage-style stations. A copper tile top and base on the large front bay window matched the copper awning over the main entrance. Flower boxes, rounded brickwork over the door and another window, wrought-iron metalwork, and decorative shutters further enhanced the warm and domestic appearance of Ott's new station. The cottage architecture and imagery were continued in the brick walls, tile roofs, gable ends, and multi-pane windows and doors throughout the complex.

In order to stay competitive in the 1930s, gas retailers began servicing automobiles. This remodeled station featured three service bays and a brand-new hoist; the drain pit, a remnant from the site's first station, was for grease jobs. Three new employees were hired before the opening to help pump gas and service and repair automobiles. The large front windows neatly displayed the latest accessories, batteries, and tires, and racks of motor oil edged the driveway. Motorists could "Drive in and be sure with Pure."

Several different operators continued to offer Pure Oil gasoline and service until the station permanently closed in 1962. The Pure Oil Company sold the building, which was later remodeled for retail and service use. The gas pumps were removed in the mid-1960s. Remarkably, this picturesque cottage station currently stands relatively intact. Its designation as a City of La Crosse historic landmark has protected it from threats of demolition.

Attendants at the English Cottage–style Pure Oil station. **Courtesy of Dennis Reeck**

WHS Accession 2008/088, photo by Mark Fay

Visit
La Crosse's
NEW
"SHOPPING
CENTER"
FOR MOTORISTS

ENJOY COMPLETE SERVICE

From Bumper-To-Bumper

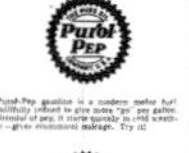

Tiolene

This attractive station, conveniently located at the corner of Fourth and Cass streets, is now open and ready to serve you. Here, amid attractive surroundings that make automotive shopping a pleasure, the complete needs of your car can be supplied at one stop.

You are cordially invited to visit this new station during our formal opening Saturday and Sunday, inspect its modern facilities, and enjoy prompt, courteous service. The local men in attendance are proud of their station, proud of the products which they sell. Drive in and be sure with Pure.

PURE SYSTEM of LUBRICATION
YALE TIRES and TUBES
PURE BATTERIES
PURE ACCESSORIES
Enclosed Facilities for Cars and Trucks

HENRY OTT'S
PURE OIL
SERVICE STATION
Fourth and Cass Sts.
LA CROSSE

La Crosse Tribune, October 22, 1937

6 Mineral Point

110 South Chestnut Street

Before 1925, automobile owners in Mineral Point could buy gasoline and oil at several locations, including auto and implement dealerships and a curbside pump on High Street, the town's main thoroughfare. However, there were no proper filling stations until Josiah Paynter built the city's first one at the corner of Chestnut and Fountain streets.

This small, prefabricated station was manufactured by the Milwaukee Corrugating Company and shipped west in sections. Also known as Milcor, the company manufactured all types of metal building products, from ventilators for barns and metal lath to gutters and ornamental cornices. Grange and Paynter Hardware of Mineral Point pieced together the Spanish tile-style metal roof and Milcor sheet-metal walls on-site, likely following a set of enclosed instructions.

In addition to being more affordable, prefabricated stations could be easily dismantled and moved elsewhere if business fell off. This was an important concern in the early days of gas retailing because highways often changed routes as roads were improved and paved. What was once a busy intersection might quickly become an unprofitable one.

Josiah Paynter ran the station from 1925 until his death in 1934, after which time his grandson, Chester Owens, operated it. In addition to washing, polishing, and greasing, Owens offered free crankcase service—despite the lack of an enclosed service bay.

The station carried Cities Service Oils and dispensed gasoline from two hand-operated gasoline pumps until 1940, when the station closed because of wartime rationing. Even though gasoline hasn't been sold at this station since 1940, the building still stands and is used for storage.

The Owens family stayed in the business, however, opening another station in town that is currently operated by Todd Owens, a great-great-grandson of Josiah Paynter.

This Milcor prefabricated station, featuring the company's distinctive metal-tile roof, could be disassembled and moved if business lagged. Courtesy of Marilyn Owens

WHS Accession 2008/088, photo by Mark Fay

Monroe

1323 Ninth Street

Clarence "Slim" Freitag's new Pure Oil service station created a sensation in 1935 when the local newspaper announced that "an attractive new brick station, finished in white and blue, has been completed. It is of unusual design, with high peaked roof and weathered copper trim."[3]

Slim was a big-band trombonist and a pilot who gave flying lessons to several Pure Oil Company executives. After his father, Henry, lost part of an ownership in an automobile sales dealership, Slim bought a corner lot and built this sixteen thousand-dollar station for his father.

The quaint English Cottage-style station with its bright blue tile roof was built according to the standard corporate design created by company architect Carl A. Petersen. The domestic appearance of the station allowed it to be easily integrated into its location on the edge of a quiet residential neighborhood about three blocks from the city square. This station represents the basic standardized plan and could easily be expanded for larger lots, as was the case with the Pure Oil station in La Crosse. Larger stations simply began with the cottage-style station at the core, and additions—service bays (Pure Oil referred to them as "Lubridomes") and showrooms—were completed with similar rooflines, materials, and, of course, the blue-and-white paint scheme.

In addition to selling Pure Oil Pep, Ethyl, and Excel gasolines, Henry Freitag marketed tires and batteries and serviced and oiled automobiles in the Lubridome service bay addition. Several individuals operated the Pure Oil station after Henry passed away in the mid-1940s. Simon Meyer ran it from the early 1950s until the 1970s. Shortly after becoming a Union 76 station, the station closed. It has housed a water-conditioning business for the past two decades.

The domestic-style Monroe Pure Oil station, designed to resemble an English cottage. Courtesy of Keith A. Sculle

Freitag's Pure Oil Service Station was added to the National Register of Historic Places in 1980 as an example of early-twentieth-century architecture used as a commercial marketing technique and corporate symbol. Even its downspouts were embossed with the Pure Oil monogram.

Collection of Mark Speltz

WHS Accession 2008/088, photo by Mark Fay

8 Platteville

340 South Chestnut Street

As the number of automobiles grew, more and more gas stations were constructed to handle the increasing sales. In the early 1930s, there were approximately fifteen gas stations serving consumers in Platteville, and one person out of four owned an automobile, according to the city's clerk. Interestingly enough, only one out of fifty-five people still owned a horse.

While it's not surprising that most of these early Platteville stations are no longer standing, one has stood the test of time and is even still used as a gas station. Built around 1930 at the corner of Chestnut and Court (Southwest Road today) streets, this little brick filling station resembled the house-with-canopy-type station commonly constructed throughout the state. The floor plan included the operator's space and restrooms. Large windows allowed plenty of light into the office. The ring of lights under the canopy illuminated the pump island and apron after dark.

The station has sold Standard, Shell, and Phillips 66 products through the years and has had a number of owners. Currently, Burt Nodorft and his son Tom run the little station as B&B's Service Station. In addition to pump sales, an important part of their business is a fuel-delivery service.

A more modern station, complete with service bays, would not fit on this compact lot, which might explain why the small filling station has not been rebuilt or replaced. The fact that the station is still being used in 2008 for its original purpose is likely due to its neighborhood-appropriate design, personal service, adequate traffic, and a good bit of perseverance by the owners—not to mention the free piece of candy customers are welcome to help themselves to after paying for their gas inside.

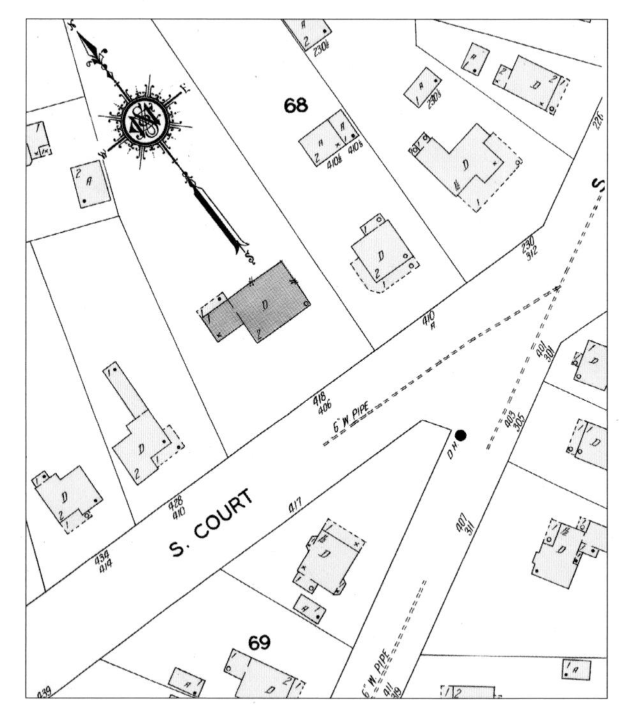

The tiny size of this corner lot, as seen in this Sanborn Fire Insurance map, ca. 1929 to 1938, shows why the small station has never been enlarged. WHi Image ID 57266

WHS Accession 2008/088, photo by Mark Fay

Gas pump globe.
Northwoods Petroleum Museum, photo by Joel Heiman

9 Prairie du Sac

105 Water Street

When Felix Ohrlein decided to build a gas station in Prairie du Sac, he contracted with the Madison-based Trachte Brothers Company, known for its prefabricated service stations. Trachte had pioneered the technique of using corrugated steel rolled out from a machine to construct garages and industrial buildings. (They originally developed their patented corrugating machine to produce livestock watering troughs.) By standing the panels on end and joining them together, they created distinctive vertical panels with horizontal ribs that were bolted together and topped with a barrel-vaulted roof. Trachte buildings were marketed as easy to assemble, and, if a location proved less than optimal, they were easy to reassemble in a new location. According to company literature, Trachte provided practical stations "in which the capital investment is cut to a minimum without sacrificing desirable essentials. Economical, portable, durable, attractive."[4]

Built in 1944–45, the station is still in use. Its false facade hides the barrel-vaulted roof. Trachte matched the styling of the station when it returned around 1963 to construct the two-bay service garage.

The current owner, Dick Ambrose, started at the station when he was sixteen and has been there ever since. Dick, his father, and Warren Witwen, who delivered fuel from the station to farmers and commercial accounts, bought the station in 1972, and Midway Oil Co. was born.

The brand of gasoline may have changed countless times since the 1940s, but this station's attendants still check the oil and tires and wash windshields while filling customers' tanks. Dick believes the full-service it offers helps set Midway Oil apart from local competitors and keeps satisfied customers coming back.

Another prefabricated Trachte Brothers gas station. This Pennco station was located on Atwood in Madison. Courtesy of O. J. Thompto

WHS Accession 2008/088, photo by Mark Fay

10 Rockbridge

1082 Lodge Street

When county surveyors plotted a new route for State Trunk Highway 80 in the fall of 1925, everyone in the village of Rockbridge was eager to know where it would be located. By June 1926, a large crew was busy building a road that would provide better year-round access to the community.

The importance of reliable transportation and roads was not lost on John and Perina Cunningham, who operated a small store and the village post office out of their Rockbridge residence. In 1926, the Cunninghams added a small filling station to the corner of their lot on Main Street (Lodge Street today) at the intersection of the new State Trunk Highway 80. John built the one-story station for his son, Floyd. The small structure had a door with a window on each side and a small canopy that provided cover for one automobile to fill up. It was clad in clapboard siding, mirroring the material of the Cunninghams' main residence.

When this station was built, there was at least one garage in town that sold gasoline. But this new filling station provided other conveniences, too. Customers could now pick up their mail, a few groceries, and a gallon or two of gas in one stop. Many gas retailers in the 1920s were able to use innovative and experimental setups like this, especially in rural areas of the state, before standardized and efficient floor plans became the norm. The tight layout on the corner lot likely dictated the unusual placement of the canopy, which would typically cover the main entrance.

Locally, the Cunninghams' filling station was known as the Mobil station even though it was leased by the Perfect Oil Company for a few years in the 1930s. It closed around 1963; the pumps and tanks were removed in the 1970s.

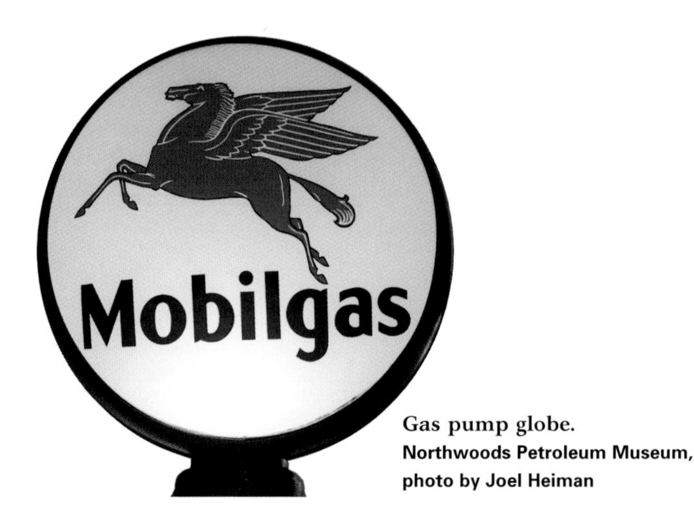

Gas pump globe.
Northwoods Petroleum Museum, photo by Joel Heiman

WHS Accession 2008/088, photo by Mark Fay

11 South Lancaster

7697 Hurricane Road

The small unincorporated community of Hurricane (located in the town of South Lancaster in Grant County) is now but a shadow of the bustling place it once was. In the early 1900s, its general store, mills, and blacksmith shop brought farmers and shoppers in from the surrounding countryside.

The community's Kerr General Store has a long history. The first store on the site was started about 1840; it was rebuilt after an 1877 fire. Samuel Kerr bought the business in 1891, beginning a service that would last almost three-quarters of a century. His store handled mail and supplied residents with sugar, flour, molasses, ground coffee, candy, and everything else from pitchforks to shotguns.

As was common in many rural communities where no one was willing to build a gas station at a small crossroads, the general store in Hurricane became the place to fill an automobile tank and purchase oil. Kerr installed a very early pump model outside the large storefront windows. He later added a second model, one that registered the gallons pumped and tallied the price.

Just as the automobile tended to end the livelihood of blacksmith and livery businesses, the ability to travel farther by automobile to communities with specialty or grocery stores also contributed to the demise of rural country stores like the Kerr General Store. Kerr's daughter, Belva Birch, ran the store after he died until she passed away in 1978. The general store was closed, the large inventory was auctioned off over four days, and the long history of the store came to an end. The building is currently a private residence.

The Kerr General Store had a sideline business in gasoline with its two pumps, as was typical for country stores in areas with no dedicated filling stations. Historic Preservation Files, Wisconsin Historical Society

WHS Accession 2008/088, photo by Mark Fay

12 Spring Green

137 South Winsted Street/State Highway 23

Like many gas retailers who have long faced a wide array of pressures, the different owners of this little station in Spring Green have confronted adverse conditions ever since it was built. The story of this picturesque station aptly demonstrates what can happen to a business dependent on road traffic when the road is closed. It also shows how the design of the building endures as a marketing tool.

Constructed in 1926, this Tudor Revival cottage-style station features a centered gable above the entrance, flared eaves, and exposed rafters. The one-story structure is stone veneered with a random pattern on the front and south-facing facades. A single-bay service garage was added in 1930. The indoor oil pit has been filled in (likely to make it a safer, usable display area), but otherwise the structure has seen few alterations. It still features the original wood-and-glass door.

The Davis and Barnard filling station operated as an affiliate of Johnson Oil when it opened. While this station weathered the Depression and gas and rubber rationing during World War II, it was ultimately a route change that spelled its demise. It went out of business after only twenty years.

Station locations were carefully chosen based on traffic patterns, but profitable locations could change overnight as new highway systems were developed and routes of travel changed. When the bridge over the nearby Wisconsin River was out of service in 1946, causing traffic to be routed elsewhere, several stations along this stretch of Highway 23 were forced to close. Today, planners craft business-retention plans as part of construction projects in the hope of mitigating such negative effects.

After closing in 1946, the former filling station was used as a weigh station for farm animals. It has seen several tenants since then. The station's third owner, Karen Davidson, bought it in 2000 to house her jewelry business. The building is currently for sale.

The pumps out front are gone now, and the palette of the painted wood trim is likely more colorful than the original, but otherwise, little has changed since the station was built. In fact, Davidson's marketing efforts—from postcards to signs to her Web site—build upon the station's image, feel, and design, much the same way the original owners hoped to attract automobilists off the highway with the station's welcoming domestic-style architecture.

WHS Accession 2008/088, photo by Mark Fay

Station attendant Louis Thering takes advantage of a lull in business. Courtesy of Jim Thering

13 Stoddard

201 North Main Street

In 1933, Lester Proksch constructed this striking filling station in the small river town of Stoddard, south of La Crosse. The station was notable for its decorative brickwork laid in a mix of standard, herringbone, and checkered patterns. The tabbed stonework around the entrance, decorative half-timbering, and a steeply pitched roof added to the homey feel of the two-story structure. Proksch, a carpenter and mason, built much of the well-crafted station himself at a cost of seventeen hundred dollars.

Interestingly, Proksch chose to construct a very domestic-style station despite the fact that many new stations being built at the time had begun to reflect the more efficient and standardized box-type station. Perhaps the station's location along Main Street in the middle of Stoddard influenced Proksch's decision to go with a design that would be acceptable and reassuring to the community.

Proksch opened Less's Service in July 1933. He placed his initials in a diamond-shaped block above the doorway and lived upstairs. Standard Oil products were sold from three pumps out front, each with a Standard crown globe on top. Subsequent owners added two service bays for greasing and repairs.

Several owners operated the station after World War II, including Theran Russell, Butch Haugerson, and Sam Pedretti in the late 1950s. Pedretti ran the station for nearly thirty years before selling it around 1990 to Marty Bauer, who operated a tire shop out of it before converting the quaint cottage-style station into an office for a realty business.

An early image shows the station before its service bay addition. **Courtesy of Ervin and Marilyn Bankes**

Note service bay at right. **Courtesy of Marty Bauer**

WHS Accession 2008/088, photo by Mark Fay

WHS Accession 2008/088, photo by Mark Fay

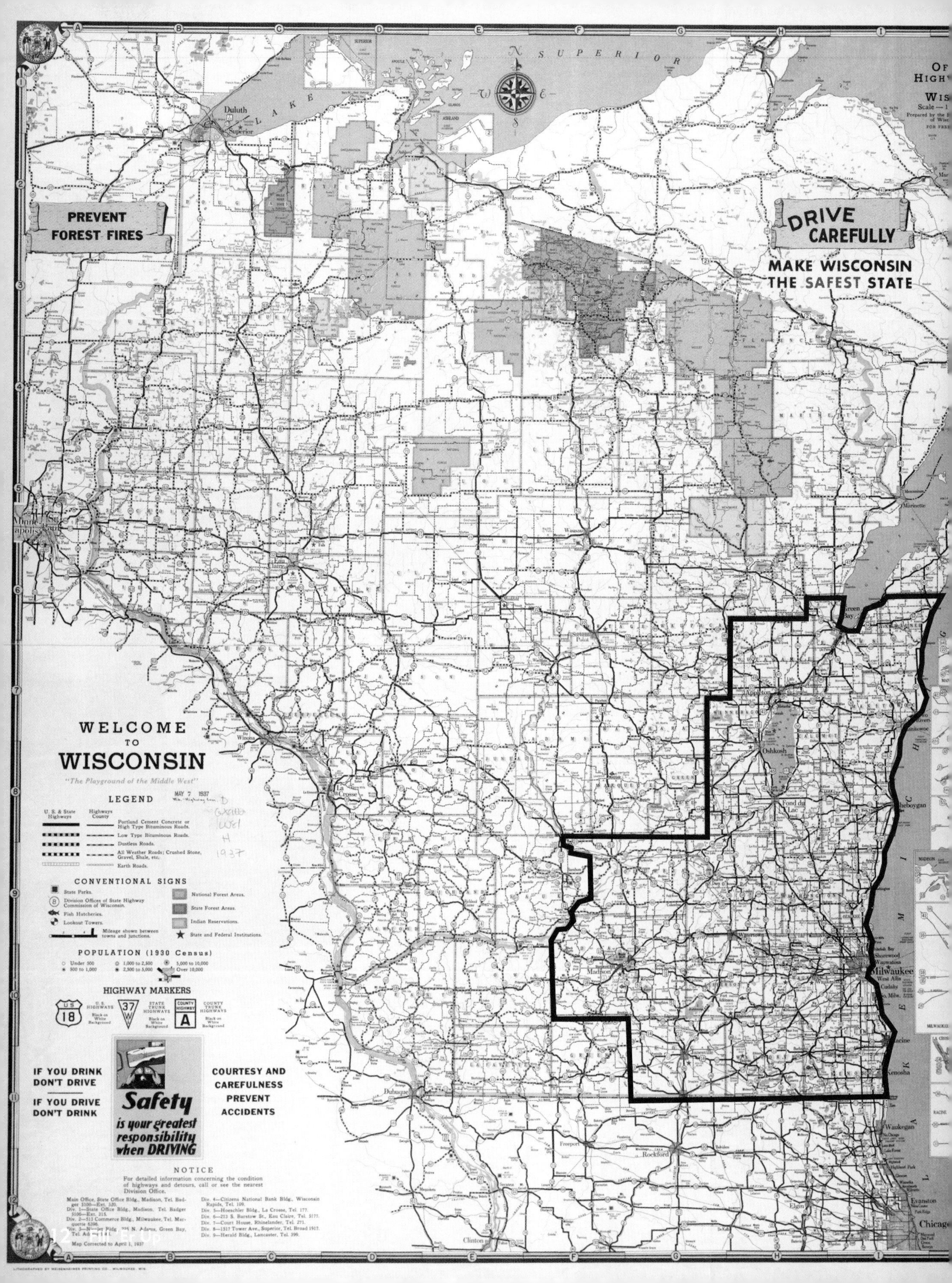

LAKE SUPERIOR
PREVENT FOREST FIRES
DRIVE CAREFULLY
MAKE WISCONSIN THE SAFEST STATE
Duluth
Superior
Ironwood
Wausau
Eau Claire
Stevens Point
Green Bay
Appleton
Oshkosh
Fond du Lac
Sheboygan
Marinette
Winona
La Crosse
Madison
Milwaukee
Racine
Kenosha
Janesville
Dubuque
Freeport
Rockford
Clinton
Elgin
Waukegan
Evanston
Chicago
WELCOME TO WISCONSIN
"The Playground of the Middle West"
MAY 7 1937
LEGEND
U. S. & State Highways
Highways County
Portland Cement Concrete or High Type Bituminous Roads.
Low Type Bituminous Roads.
Dustless Roads.
All Weather Roads; Crushed Stone, Gravel, Shale, etc.
Earth Roads.
CONVENTIONAL SIGNS
State Parks.
Division Offices of State Highway Commission of Wisconsin.
Fish Hatcheries.
Lookout Towers.
Mileage shown between towns and junctions.
National Forest Areas.
State Forest Areas.
Indian Reservations.
State and Federal Institutions.
POPULATION (1930 Census)
Under 500
500 to 1,000
1,000 to 2,500
2,500 to 5,000
5,000 to 10,000
Over 10,000
HIGHWAY MARKERS
US 18
U. S. HIGHWAYS
Black on White Background
37 W
STATE TRUNK HIGHWAYS
Black on White Background
COUNTY HIGHWAY A
COUNTY TRUNK HIGHWAYS
Black on White Background
IF YOU DRINK DON'T DRIVE
IF YOU DRIVE DON'T DRINK
Safety is your greatest responsibility when DRIVING
COURTESY AND CAREFULNESS PREVENT ACCIDENTS
NOTICE
For detailed information concerning the condition of highways and detours, call or see the nearest Division Office.
Main Office, State Office Bldg., Madison, Tel. Badger 5100—Ext. 320.
Div. 1—State Office Bldg., Madison. Tel. Badger 5100—Ext. 315.
Div. 2—513 Commerce Bldg., Milwaukee, Tel. Marquette 6398.
Div. 4—Citizens National Bank Bldg., Wisconsin Rapids, Tel. 109.
Div. 5—Hoeschler Bldg., La Crosse, Tel. 177.
Div. 6—213 S. Barstow St., Eau Claire, Tel. 5177.
Div. 7—Court House, Rhinelander, Tel. 271.
Div. 8—1517 Tower Ave., Superior, Tel. Broad 1917.
Div. 9—Herald Bldg., Lancaster, Tel. 399.
Map Corrected to April 1, 1937

EAST

14 Burlington
15 Cedarburg
16 Town of Emmet
17 Fond du Lac
18 Glendale
19 Hartland
20 Janesville—Sinclair
21 Janesville—Standard
22 Jefferson
23 Kenosha
24 Kewaunee
25 Madison—Clark
26 Madison—Edwards Super Service Station
27 Madison—Parman's Super Service Station
28 Madison—Severson's Service Station
29 Madison—Shell
30 Manitowoc
31 Mequon
32 Milwaukee
33 Muskego
34 Genoa City
35 Oshkosh
36 Pulaski
37 Stoughton
38 Waterford—Wadhams
39 Waterford—Phillips
40 Watertown
41 West Allis

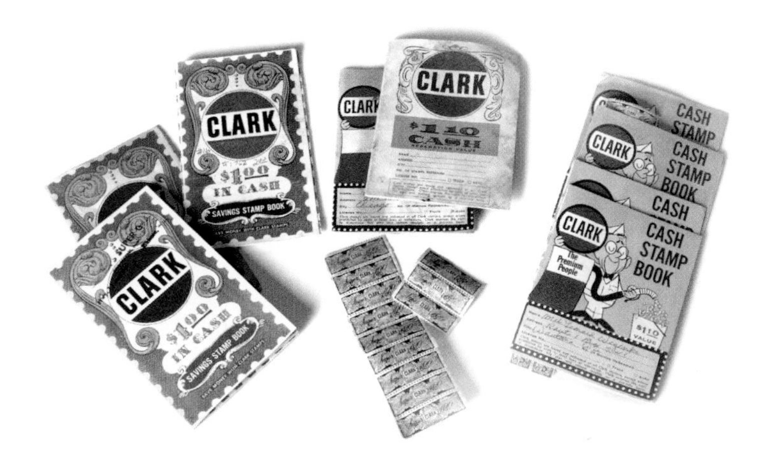

14 Burlington

148 West Chestnut Street

Early automobilists passing through Burlington in the first two decades of the twentieth century would have filled their tanks at pumps in front of hardware stores and garages downtown, or at bulk plants on the edge of town. It wasn't until 1927 that Jack Hansen built the community's first filling station, locating the structure with a brick facade painted white immediately behind the business district, at the corner of Chestnut and Mill streets.

The small station was set back on the corner lot and placed diagonally so motorists could conveniently approach from both streets. With its Colonial influences, brown brick side walls, and roof tiles (which were fireproof), it was welcoming in a way that the other, more utilitarian spots to fill up in Burlington were not.

Motorists surely looked around in wonder while they gassed up for the first time at the new filling station. Raised parapet end walls were topped with arched chimney hoods, stone coping, and classical-style urns. Specially arranged night lighting illuminated the station. The Hansen Oil Company placed a Western Union clock, noted as "the only outdoor timepiece in the business section of the city," above the door.[5]

Hansen Oil Company boasted about the station's up-to-date service machinery, including an electric lift for oil changing and greasing, and a car-washing platform. Seven pumps set on islands in the crushed-limestone driveway dispensed Nevr-Nox, which, according to the company's promotional materials, "gives Pep, Power, and Long Mileage."

Hansen Oil was a member of Dixie Distributors, a statewide affiliation of independent operators who used the Dixie colors, design, marketing, and bulk purchasing power to compete against the industry giants. The Burlington station's pumps displayed the blue-and-yellow Dixie Distributors colors and bore its insignia.

By the mid-1930s, Hansen Oil carried a full line of Skelly Oil Company products. Around this time, Jack Hansen hired Beulah Wolline as manager and bookkeeper. She even pumped gas. After Hansen died in 1954, Wolline ran the business for the next thirty years under the ownership of Hansen's widow. When she passed away, Wolline became the owner. The pumps were stopped in 1990 because of the high projected expense of updating the underground storage tanks to meet the stringent state-mandated regulations. Hansen Oil still maintains this quaint cottage as a storage building.

ca. 1976.
Courtesy of Burlington Historical Society

WHS Accession 2008/088, photo by Mark Fay

Introducing—
DICK SEE

"Howdy, Folks, I'm mighty glad to meet all of you. For the next year I'm going to be a frequent visitor in your home through the medium of this newspaper. I've got only one thing to talk about—our Town—for I'm livin' right here in Burlington now. I'll be busy all the time just seein' and talkin' about things and maybe I can be of some help in tellin' you things you haven't time to observe.

"We've got a real town here and if we don't appreciate it we can't expect anyone else to. So let's get acquainted. In the meantime if you're looking for a real gasoline value try DIXIE GOLDEN—that quick startin', more mileage fuel."

DICK SEE.

Follow the adventures of Dick See every week through this column and have your crankcase filled with Dixis Super Motor Oil for perfect summer lubrication.

Hansen Oil Co.

Burlington, Wis.

Burlington Standard Democrat, June 1, 1934

I See "Dick See"

A Burlington man found accidental fame in 1934 because of his resemblance to Dixie Oil's new mascot. When the cartoon man, "Dick See," was unveiled at a Dixie Distributors' meeting, Jack Hansen, owner of a Hansen Oil gas station, noted the resemblance to Burlington local Tom Warren.

Later, a photo of Warren, posing as "Dick," graced the cover of the oil company's *National Dixie Booster* magazine. Inside, a brief bio declared: "He is a droll old fellow, as honest as the day is long, with the love of a good story, the ability to observe pertinently, whose good nature and easy going ways make him really loveable." Warren was an excellent human representative of "Dick," a lovable old cartoon man who had many friends and always knew what was going on in his small town.[1]

Notes

1. "Tom Warren Poses as Likeness to 'Dick See,' Dixie Oil Character," *Burlington Standard Democrat*, May 18, 1934; "Introducing Dick See" (advertisement), *Burlington Standard Democrat*, June 1, 1934.

15 Cedarburg

N58W6189 Columbia Road

Driving through the historic town of Cedarburg, its downtown streets lined with handsome nineteenth-century stone buildings, the last thing one would expect to see is a Japanese pagoda complete with Japanese lanterns suspended from it. Set next to a colossal Civil War–era mill, the former Wadhams service station warrants a second look.

Well-known Milwaukee architect Alexander C. Eschweiler designed the exotic station for the Wadhams Oil and Grease Company of Milwaukee in 1926. His groundbreaking designs for the company captured the excitement and adventure of travel. Eschweiler's innovation was imagining architectural design as a marketing device: the pagoda became yet another piece of corporate imagery, joining gas pumps, signs, logos, and other devices in imprinting the corporate identity on the customer. Upon seeing the bright red metal tile roof with its flared eaves, motorists immediately knew they were approaching a Wadhams station.

ca. 1950s. Courtesy of Kay Walters

When it opened, this station featured women's and men's restrooms and office space. Two large plate-glass windows showcased products available for sale. Multi-pane windows spanned the length of the two sides of the structure. In the back, a sizable garage space with a pit and, later, a hoist, allowed for greasing, car washing, and other services.

Known as Billy's Service Station, the structure was built for William Schnabel. Although it rained nonstop on opening day, November 13, 1926, 288 curious motorists pulled through the pumps and purchased 1,805 gallons of Wadhams gasoline.

The station continues to be owned by the Schnabel family. William's daughter, Kay Walters, the current owner, spent much of her childhood there. One of her fondest memories is playing on a swing that her father hung from the garage hoist, which he designed and built himself.

More than one hundred of these eye-catching Wadhams stations were built in Wisconsin between 1917 and 1930, but only a handful of them remain. This unique structure, which now houses a jewelry shop, is on the National Register of Historic Places as part of Cedarburg's Washington Avenue Historic District.

Courtesy of Kay Walters

Your account stated to date. If error is found return at once.

Billy's Service Station

GAS, OILS, AUTO ACCESSORIES

Cedarburg, Wis., 9/25 1940

M Cedarburg Marble Co

Address

Reg. No. Clerk ACCOUNT FORWARDED 4.00

1	5 Gal Motor	1.00
2		5.00
3	Fred Kirschman	
4		
5		
6	Paid 10/14/40	
7		
8	Billy	
9		
10		
11		
12	23	

Interest charged on all bills after 60 days.

WHS Accession 2008/088, photo by Mark Fay

Playful image of a toy plane stopping by for fuel.
Courtesy of Kay Walters

16 Town of Emmet

N1085 Highway 26

This little station, located close to the intersection of Highways 16 and 26 north of Watertown, was built in the mid-1920s. Constructed of red brick and capped by a steeply pitched gable roof accented with gently flared eaves, this one-story station resembled an English cottage. The clock that still can be seen in the front gable over the entrance was a common design element in stations of the period.

The station originally featured an operator's office lit by sunlight streaming through the large front and side windows; it also included a small attic and basement. A door to the women's restroom was outside, around the back, while the men's room—which would have been shared with the station attendants—was accessible from the inside. Three pumps, topped with glass Standard crown globes, originally sat out front. An outdoor oil pit was to the side of the building.

The Slight family leased the station from Standard Oil Company before eventually purchasing it as part of their business catering to highway travelers and tourists: they owned a dozen or more cabins behind the station. Despite the size of the picturesque white cabins, which were even smaller than the seven-hundred-square-foot station, they were a popular form of tourist accommodations before motels became common.

The cabins are gone now, but the tourist-camp bathhouse remains along with the station, which stopped selling gasoline and closed in the 1950s. It's currently used as office space.

WHS Accession 2008/088, photo by Mark Fay

17 Fond du Lac

115 North Main Street

Located in Fond du Lac along the city's gasoline alley (so called because of the concentration of gas stations, auto dealerships, and service garages along the road), this one-story service station was built in the mid-1930s by Clark Oil Company (a separate company from Emory T. Clark's chain). The Art Deco stylings—openings flanked by fluted pilasters, three shaped parapets along the top of the facade—were likely chosen to impress and attract customers by associating the modern convenience of auto travel with the popular style seen in movies.

The builders constructed the station with concrete block, which, because it was inexpensive, fire resistant, lightweight, durable, and easy to work with, became a preferred material for stations of this era. Art Deco design suited these new stations because the simple, abstract, geometric ornament could be easily and inexpensively cast in concrete block faces.

Despite the impressive design and efficient layout of this station, Clark Oil sold or leased it out to others after just a few years. For the next twenty years, the station's name and operators changed six times until it became the home of City Taxi in the early 1960s. The large station houses a locksmithing business today.

WHS Accession 2008/088, photo by Mark Fay

WHS Accession 2008/088, photo by Mark Fay

18 Glendale

7575 North Port Washington Road

Phillips Petroleum gambled on a planned expressway interchange when it built this station in Glendale in 1966. The building itself, with its spirited architecture, bold colors, and soaring canopy, was bound to attract attention. But when the interchange was scrapped, so, too, were the plans for high sales volume.

The standardized design of this station was developed by Clarence Reinhardt, a Phillips company architect who sought to create a distinctive look, one based on midcentury culture and design. Reinhardt hoped to translate the sweeping angular forms of the period, as seen in drive-ins and the tail fins of Cadillacs, into a new, striking design for Phillips.

The slanted windows of the office and display area cut the reflection of headlight glare and also increased the visibility of the interior. Set at an angle away from the pump islands, the service doors and pump locations were strategically placed to improve safety and traffic flow. Two red harlequins—diamond-like symbols—were painted on the wall between the service doors, representing another Phillips logo that also could be found on charge cards, promotional giveaways, and even drinking glasses sold at stations. Those with this new look came to be known as Harlequin stations.

The Glendale station's distinctive canopy is rare today as many Phillips stations were closed, sold off, or drastically altered. Bob Peter and his sister, Karen, own the station their father originally leased in 1969, and they are proud of the station's unique and remarkably intact design.

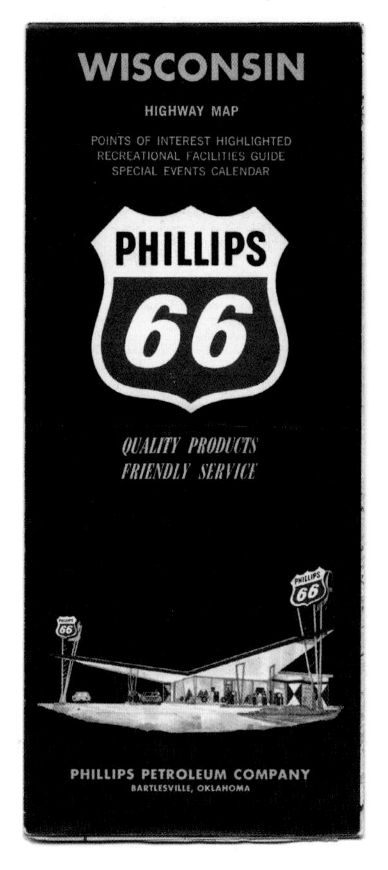

An example of the dramatic double-canopy "batwings" of another Phillips station adorned the company's 1963 road map. Collection of Mark Speltz

WHS Accession 2008/088, photo by Mark Fay

19 Hartland

252–256 West Capitol Drive

In the first decades of the twentieth century, successful filling-station designs had not yet been standardized, so creative entrepreneurs looking to get into the gas-retailing business could take a chance on an unorthodox design. Some people, in the name of economy, opened filling stations in existing structures designated for other uses—sometimes even their homes. The Trapp Filling Station, located in Hartland, was one such unusual example of a combined-use station.

The Tudor Revival–style structure was built as a residence in the early 1920s but altered by the Trapp family a few years later to also house a filling station in the lower story; in the 1930s, they added a single service bay. The two-story structure featured a stone foundation and an upper story clad in stucco and decorative half-timbering. A free-standing stone arch to the left of the facade complemented the structure's overall design.

Cornelius Trapp's station was situated along the community's major highway. But despite the high volume of traffic, the station soon closed. A succession of grocery stores and other commercial establishments followed; it's currently a private residence. The Trapp Filling Station was added to the National Register of Historic Places in 1986 as a noteworthy example of Tudor Revival design, one that combined a residence and service station.

ca. 1950s.
Courtesy of Hartland Historical Society

WHS Accession 2008/088, photo by Mark Fay

20 Janesville—Sinclair

720 Center Avenue

Built in 1925 by A. J. O'Donnell at a cost of five hundred dollars, this Janesville filling station was designed to resemble a house—albeit one that measured only two hundred square feet. Large windows flanked each side of the main entrance, and the steeply pitched roof with a centered gable added to this filling station's quaint cottage look.

Just outside of the front entrance were two large gas pumps that originally sold Wadhams products. An outdoor pit allowed for grease jobs and oil changes, although automobile services were secondary to the gasoline business. O'Donnell sold the station to Ivol Fairfield by 1934. It was known as Fairfield Service Station until about 1960.

Beginning in 1960, Bob Hedgecock owned and operated the station, selling oil, candy, and even bait from the tiny building. The extension of credit to regular customers and full-service at the pumps had guaranteed a stream of regulars for many years—enough to enable Hedgecock to support a family of nine. But in 1977, cost-cutting competition from self-service stations and increased costs from credit card fees combined to force him to close.

Bob Tracey, whose family's roots in the oil and gasoline business in Janesville date to the 1920s, purchased the property in the late 1990s and placed vintage pumps out front. The small building's styling eventually inspired the design of the large convenience store directly behind it. The use of stucco, a similar roofline, and a small window within the gabled peak visually connected the two structures. Yet a quick comparison of the stations—the large number of pumps out front and the massive amount of products inside the new station are particularly noteworthy—reveals how the gas-retailing industry has changed since the 1920s. Now used for storage, the little station stands as a reminder of a time of service and filling stations long past.

This tiny cottage-style station is now overshadowed by the larger convenience store its design inspired. Photo by Jim Draeger

WHS Accession 2008/088, photo by Mark Fay

All in a Day's Work

Bob Hedgecock in his station, ca. 1963.
Courtesy of Bob Hedgecock

"In the summer hours, the fishing season, I'd wake up at five o'clock in the morning and get the neighbor boy and we'd go out in the country and [catch] minnows at one of the creeks out there and we'd get back about seven or so and...sort out the minnows according to size. Then at eight o'clock I'd open up and I'd pump gas, sometimes in my hip boots yet. Then...after the first rush was over, around nine o'clock, my wife would bring my breakfast over and I'd have breakfast. Sometimes she'd stay and eat with me. And...then after that, I'd do things like grease jobs and tire repairs that I'd made time for, you know. Then in the afternoon, when school let out and work let out, why...kids would start showing up and then people start showing up for gas and stuff like that. That's kinda the way my day went, then in the evening after I closed, I'd go home and my wife and I...[would] enjoy a supper together. After I watched the news on TV, I'd go out and hunt night crawlers, sometimes 'til midnight. That was a pretty long day." —*Bob Hedgecock, former owner/operator of the Sinclair station at 720 Center Avenue, Janesville*[1]

Notes

1. Bob Hedgecock, interview by David Hestad, Wisconsin Public Television, June 13, 2006.

21 Janesville—Standard

101 North Franklin

In an effort to take full advantage of a successful location and consolidate a number of automobile-related activities under one roof, Standard Oil Company constructed this brick super-service station in 1930 at the corner of North Franklin and Wall streets in Janesville.

Standard Oil demolished the station—one of the city's earliest—originally on this site and spent twelve thousand dollars (more than double the cost of an average home at the time) to build its upgraded and expanded replacement. Its Spanish Colonial–style details included decorative tile insets and red-clay-tile, shed-roofed parapets that evoked the tile roofs typical of Spanish Colonial homes.

In addition to dispensing gas, the L-shaped building also housed a sizable showroom for tire and battery sales as well as an up-to-date, one-stop shop for automobile repairs and service. Competitive pressures and the sour economy of the Depression forced gas retailers to try to increase sales of tires, batteries, and accessories to keep a business going. This station's large display windows showed off the newest product lines, beckoning motorists to come inside to have a look. It was hoped that increased visibility and promotion would lead to greater revenues.

Retailers also sought to offer more reliable service, which they hoped would reflect well upon Standard Oil, increase gas sales, and provide the station with a competitive edge. The company offered virtually any service needed for an automobile, from greasing to washing, and sold parts ranging from brakes to tires. The service bays were outfitted with the newest equipment, including machines for charging batteries and repairing tire tubes. They featured hydraulic lifts, instead of the usual pits, and were heated in the winter.

Except for a few years in the late 1970s when it sat vacant, this super-service station has housed tire- and automobile-related businesses throughout its existence. In the early 1980s, H&H Automotive set up shop in the old Standard Oil station and has continued operations there for more than twenty years.

The building, which survived a threatened demolition in 2002 to make way for a new police station, still stands as a rare intact example of the Standard Oil Company's standardized design for its super-service stations. It is eligible for listing on the National Register of Historic Places, but, as of early 2008, its future is once again in question.

WHS Accession 2008/088, photo by Mark Fay

Standard Oil glass gas pump globe.
WHS Museum 1998.20.160

22 Jefferson

109 North Center Avenue

By the time Sylvester "Sal" Spangler built this station in 1935, he had already owned and worked at several service stations in Jefferson. He understood it would be his friendly and superior service that would bring in customers and keep them loyal for the next thirty-five years.

One year after opening with Conoco in the pumps, Spangler switched his own allegiance to Standard Oil products. He recognized the power of loyalty when he took out newspaper ads reassuring customers that "Mr. Spangler will continue to offer the same brand of cheerful service and wishes to have the opportunity of serving you."[6]

Located on Center Avenue, near Racine Street, the station originally consisted of a single tiny filling station containing an office. Spangler painted the low-cost concrete block structure white. Its Art Deco–inspired crenellated parapets were added to evoke an image of modernity. The large plate-glass window, which originally had a row of five small transom lights above, displayed cans of motor oil and other accessories. Several years later, Spangler constructed a second separate building south of the original filling station, with parapets to match the original.

The deep setback from the street allowed for automotive access to both sides of the pumps and accommodated the growing promotion of automotive accessories such as tires from Atlas and, later, Firestone. Gerald "Jerry" Probst took over management of Spangler's Service Station in 1970, carrying Shell products. Spangler eventually sold the building in 1981 to Lyle Punzel, who closed the station in the late 1980s, when new tanks were needed.

Late 2007.
WHS Accession 2008/088, photo by Mark Fay

ca. 1935. **Courtesy of Jim and Phyllis Spangler**

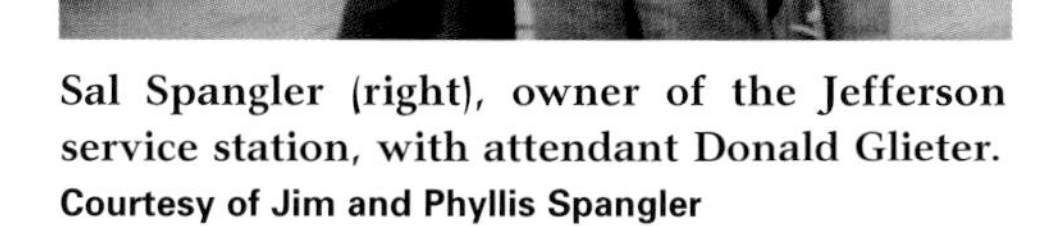

Sal Spangler (right), owner of the Jefferson service station, with attendant Donald Glieter.
Courtesy of Jim and Phyllis Spangler

ca. 1970s.
Courtesy of Jim and Phyllis Spangler

23 Kenosha

2122 Sixtieth Street

When Gregario Gallo constructed this station in Kenosha, he sought to change the common perception among motorists that gas stations were grim, dirty sheds run by unscrupulous characters. Gallo chose a Classical Revival design for his Your Choice Service Station to create an image of respectability. He anticipated that this architectural style would be attractive and acceptable to the community.

The station's classical design and features were similar to those often used on more highly regarded buildings, such as courthouses and libraries. Images of stations built to resemble Greek monuments—with rows of columns, white terra-cotta, and tile roofs—filled the pages of gas-retailing-industry magazines published in the early 1920s. Gallo may have seen this trend and employed it in the expectation that it would influence the views of Kenosha's early motorists enough to attract them to his clean station.

Built between 1923 and 1924, it incorporated concrete pilasters and an entablature with a plain frieze and raised cornice. Each of the building's three sections was topped with a brick parapet embellished with short pilasters, inset panels, and two medallions.

Gallo's station also featured an efficient layout with restrooms, an office, and a sales area for tires, tubes, and batteries. The large windows offered not only display space for merchandise but also a clear view of the driveways to ensure prompt service at the pumps. Later, a two-bay service area was discretely added around back.

Gallo's family owned the property until the late 1960s, periodically leasing the service station to other operators. The Pugh Oil Company then owned it for decades before selling it to the Uptown Business Improvement District in 1993. The new owners cleaned up and renovated the building. A flower shop has operated in the former gas station with grand ambitions since 1994.

WHS Accession 2008/088, photo by Mark Fay

24 Kewaunee

302 Ellis Street

Given the volatility of the gas-retailing business and the short life span of most gas station structures, it's remarkable that little has changed at this one in its seventy-seven years.

When this Tudor Revival–style Wadhams Service Station opened in 1931, *The Kewaunee Enterprise* proclaimed it a "very fine improvement in the business section of the city."[7] Constructed for the Salkowski brothers—Leo, Ed, and Martin—the building's red brick and stonework, coupled with the decorative half-timbering, evoked the feel of a residence. The plans came from a builder who had put up an identical station in Chicago. Motorists could seek shelter under the wide arch canopy while getting a fill-up and service at the station set on the southwestern corner of Ellis and Milwaukee streets in Kewaunee.

When this station was built, retailers and oil companies were facing increased economic pressure to generate revenues because margins and profits from gas sales alone were being pinched. While some stations at this time had one service bay or maybe two, the Salkowski brothers recognized the need to diversify, so they constructed three service bays with all of the modern equipment, including automatic lifts. The motoring public in Kewaunee could stop in for gas and also find greasing, repairs, and washing available. Business demand was so great during the station's first few weeks that its doors were opened before its spacious restrooms were completed.

Ed operated the station for many years. His son, Bob, ran it until 1976, when it was sold to Parkos Oil. Don Parkos headed up the business before handing over the reins to his son, Dean. During this period, the station's three service bays became two to accommodate later-era cars, which tended to be wider.

Gas is still being pumped at this station after nearly eight decades. The building's functional design and attractive architectural style have served its few owners well over the course of its existence.

WHS Accession 2008/088, photo by Mark Fay

WHS Accession 2008/088, photo by Mark Fay

25 Madison—Clark

1129 South Park Street

This small box gas station—the third station constructed on this corner lot—is representative of the changing models of gas retailing. In particular, it's an example of the overwhelming number of locations where stations were periodically demolished and replaced as innovations in technology and marketing changed the necessary architectural requirements to efficiently provide services. One can glimpse the broader evolution of gas retailing and station design by viewing the progression of stations at just this one location.

This station was built in 1964 by Clark Oil Company at an estimated cost of less than twelve thousand dollars. To make room for it, Clark Oil demolished Frank Moore's Pure Oil station, which featured service bays, an office, and two restrooms along with an attached restaurant. That station, opened in 1938, had replaced a Wadhams Oil filling station constructed on the same lot in 1929.

Emory T. Clark built the Midwest's largest independent oil company by concentrating on placing inexpensive, no-frills stations at high-volume locations such as this one. Constructed of concrete block, the station was a compact shed-roofed box with just restrooms, selling space, and a small storage room. The large front windows thrust up and outward toward passing motorists; the roof sloped backward.

This Madison station was designed during a time when companies such as Clark Oil were gradually shifting toward offering gasoline, motor oil, and a small selection of merchandise such as soft drinks and snacks. Clark had no interest in servicing automobiles as part of his business. He offered only premium gas at a deep discount. In the retailing industry, this station was a "high-volume pumper" and occupied a niche before the rise of self-service. Built as a full-service operation, this station eventually switched to self-serve, complete with a large canopy, with the attendant simply taking payment for the gasoline and merchandise from inside the station. There were no more friendly attendants running to the pumps and wiping windows. The days of full-service had passed.

WHS Accession 2008/088, photo by Joel Heiman

WHS Accession 2008/088, photo by Mark Fay

Northwoods Petroleum Museum,
photo by Joel Heiman

Madison—Edwards Super Service Station

202 East Washington Avenue

When Edwards Super Service Station officially opened for business on August 16, 1930, the large complex represented an effort to logically group related automobile services in one building to efficiently meet all the needs of Madison's motorists.

The complex of connected buildings—with red tile roofs and Spanish-influenced design—was designed by Harry Alford, a well-known Madison architect. Built at the corner of East Washington Avenue and Webster Street, just a block from the state capitol, the cream-colored station featured bright blue striped awnings and blue shutters and trim throughout. L. W. Burch, owner of the Electrical Supply Store located next door, erected the buildings at a cost of approximately twenty-eight thousand dollars.

Gas retailers in the early 1930s were selling less gas even as prices dropped. A greater reliance on automotive-accessory sales forced retailers to stock and display a wide array of products. Motorists filling up at Edwards Super Service could view the products and accessories such as Presto-Lite batteries through the large plate-glass windows or browse in the showroom. Racks of motor oil and tires leaned prominently against the building.

The early 1930s also saw the development of complete auto servicing. Retailers sought to provide efficient and friendly service for all vehicles, any time of day or night. This station offered greasing, wheel alignments, tire repairing, washing, and even storage space for cars.

By 1933, this station had become a Pennco service station that featured Barnsdall "Be Square" Petroleum products and Dunlop tires. While gasoline is no longer sold on this site, Pahl Tire Company set up shop in the building in the early 1960s and has been at this location for more than forty years.

ca. 1933.
WHi Image ID 17208

WHS Accession 2008/088, photo by Mark Fay

Pahl Tire Company has operated out of the building since the early 1960s. **Courtesy of Doug Pahl**

1966.
Courtesy of Doug Pahl

Madison—Parman's Super Service Station

3502 Monroe Street

Parman's Super Service Station looks almost identical to when it opened on Monroe Street in Madison more than sixty-five years ago. Built by Clayton "Clayt" Parman in 1941, the station is a prototypical example of the box-type service station that was developed in the 1930s and dominated gas station design until the 1960s.

Parman's design followed the general trend toward combining the operator's room and service bays into a rectangular boxlike structure. Clad in white stucco, the station had a flat roof and red trim that accentuated its horizontal profile. The raised vertical stripes above the main entrance and lettering were also red, exploiting the high visibility of this primary color against a white background. Parman's also made use of large windows for lighting the interior and displaying merchandise, including tires and motor oils. All of these facets became hallmarks of the box-type design, noted for its efficiency and functionality.

The Parman brothers proudly display this ad featuring their dad and the station he built. Courtesy of Clayton and Keith Parman, photo by Joel Heiman

In addition to providing prompt and full service at the four gas pumps out front, Parman's has serviced automobiles in the two well-lit service bays since its beginning. The multi-pane bay doors allow motorists to view vehicles being serviced while waiting at the pumps, a form of point-of-purchase advertising effective in promoting mechanical work.

Clayton "Junior" Parman Jr. began working at his dad's station full time in 1953, and his brother, Keith, came onboard in 1960. Despite the arrival of self-service pumps in the 1970s and the ensuing changes, the Parman brothers continued to offer full-service until they pulled their pumps in 1998 in the face of the expensive upgrades required by state law.

As of 2008, the Parman brothers are both at the station daily servicing automobiles. It used to be that regular customers would stop in frequently and fill up on conversation and gossip while getting gas. Even though the gas is gone, a small group of neighbors and friends convene at the station each morning for coffee, doughnuts, and conversation. The gentlemen refer to themselves as "lounge lizards" and try to stay out of the way as they congregate in the service bays or the front office, fondly referred to as the "sun room." These gatherings are representative of the role gas stations have long played in neighborhoods.

WHS Accession 2008/088, photo by Mark Fay

ca. 1941. **Courtesy of O. J. Thompto**

Keith and Clayton Parman. **WHS Accession 2008/088, photo by Joel Heiman**

28 Madison—Severson's Service Station

2089 Atwood Avenue

As the automobile began to influence the layout and design of American cities, gas stations gradually displaced railroad depots as informal social centers of communities. Children stopped by to fill up bike tires and buy candy. Adults gathered and shared family news and views on politics or local issues. But as neighborhood stations closed, these gathering places were lost. This was not the case, however, at 2089 Atwood Avenue, where a former Madison service station was successfully transformed into a diner.

The station, known as Severson's Service Station, was built in the early 1930s. Its International Style influence, seen most clearly in the corner windows, was favored by station designers due to its no-frills, economical design. It included a second-story office space, uncommon in most designs of the period. A large wraparound window on each floor displayed pyramids of oilcans and other merchandise for sale. A clock was set high above the main entrance, nearly even with the roofline of two service bays that were well lit by the numerous windows. The pump island out front featured four pumps dispensing Phillips 66 gasoline. Designed to showcase additional products as close as possible to customers waiting in their cars, two of the pumps contained small display cases.

Richard and Dave Havey owned and operated the station for many years but retired in the late 1980s. When Joe Krupp purchased the unique station in 1989, the concept of a diner lent itself well to the structure's sleek surfaces, modern lines, and simple form. Along with the restored Barrymore Theatre across the street, Monty's Blue Plate Diner has contributed to the reshaping of Madison's vibrant Schenk-Atwood neighborhood while continuing its tradition as a gathering place.

A party at Severson's Service Station, 1936. Note the pyramid displays of oilcans in the second-story window. WHi Image ID 3680

WHS Accession 2008/088, photo by Joel Heiman

WHS Accession 2008/088, photo by Mark Fay

This beautiful 1940s calendar hangs on the wall at Monty's Blue Plate Diner.
WHS Accession 2008/088, photo by Joel Heiman

29 Madison—Shell

950 South Park Street

When the Shell Oil Company built this service station on Madison's Park Street in 1963, the company was feeling pressure (later promoted as a Beautify America campaign by Lady Bird Johnson) to improve station aesthetics and blend the buildings into the surroundings. Shell's standardized ranch-style design reflected the company's desire to construct stations that echoed the forms and lines of what was then America's most popular single-family-house form.

This large single-story service station, which cost an estimated twenty-two thousand dollars, featured the operator's office and sales area along with three service bays. Numerous windows throughout the brick-and-wood-clad station provided a well-lit space and a viewable service area. In essence, the long, low rooflines, simple materials, and windows—ornamentation that reflected the ranch-style architecture popular elsewhere—decorated what remained underneath: the efficient box-type station.

When this station opened, its color scheme was likely Shell's beige trimmed in red—another conscious attempt to avoid the garish color schemes found in station designs of the previous decades. The long roof overhang allowed for outdoor vending and covered the entrances of the women's and men's bathrooms located side by side on the exterior.

This station is emblematic of the sweeping changes that were required as gas retailing moved toward self-service. In 1978, when a full-service station no longer proved viable at this location, it was redesigned for self-service—just fifteen years after it was built. With the servicing of autos also discontinued here, the automotive service area was repurposed into a convenience store, its service bay doors removed and the opening filled in. The station is still in use as a gas station and convenience store.

WHS Accession 2008/088, photo by Mark Fay

30 Manitowoc

908 North Eighth Street

When Clark Oil Company (not related to Emory T. Clark) announced the formal opening of its fourth station in Manitowoc, the small local company emphasized that the building's design was appropriate for a neighborhood. It was, according to one of its 1927 opening-day advertisements, "made and dressed up as we believe a service station in a residence district should be."[8]

With its graceful columns, a pedimented porch, and metal tile roof, this small brick station no doubt reflected a desire for community acceptance. Clark Oil Company decorated it further with multi-pane windows, shutters, and window boxes brimming with flowers. Female motorists strolled through a decorative trellis to access a clean, private restroom at the side of the building. Motorists received free bouquets of fresh flowers with every five gallons of gas purchased on holidays.

As the station became part of the neighborhood, boys often stopped in to catch a ball game on the radio with an early operator, Arthur Otto. They also liked to leave their neckties there on the way to school and slip them back on as they made their way home.

Yet, neighborliness and prompt service did not always ensure success and profitability. As other larger service stations were built with multiple service bays, Clark Oil Company sought to update and modernize this small station to keep it competitive. However, its efforts were frustrated in the 1940s and 1950s due to petitions and zoning concerns by the neighborhood itself. Never enlarged, this quaint station continued to sell gas, at one time as a Texaco station and later as a Spur station, before closing for good in the mid-1980s. The current owner completed an addition in 2007 and has transformed the space into a coffee and ice cream shop, hoping to make it a gathering place once again. Little of the original station has survived.

ca. 1929. **Courtesy of Paula Kohlmeier**

Late 2007. **WHS Accession 2008/088, photo by Mark Fay**

Spring 2008.
WHS Accession 2008/088, photo by Mark Fay

31 Mequon

11209 North Cedarburg Road

This contemporary station and convenience store was built in 2004 but harkens back to the early decades of the twentieth century when communities pressured oil companies for better filling-station designs that blended into neighborhoods. Small cottage-style stations, built with window boxes, ornamental ironwork, and chimneys, aimed to shed the image of grimy and unsafe oil stations. An interest in such context-sensitive design has come full circle as communities today address the appearance of their suburban fringes and the look of gas stations, franchise restaurants, and big-box retailers within those spaces.

The city of Mequon took a keen interest in this property near a gateway to the community. An effort to expand an existing gas station business prompted the city to require a design that better reflected Mequon's image. The red brick station accented with limestone evokes the image of a picturesque cottage—albeit one on a grander scale. The gabled roof is topped with a cupola. Decorative herringbone-patterned brickwork and large windows with green awnings embellish the presentation.

The most interesting aspect of the overall design is the station's placement. Unlike most stations, which boldly proclaim their function via huge, colorful signs and pumps, and large canopies facing the street, the Towne Market Mobil station tucked its pumps out back. The green spaces around the rectangular station are tastefully landscaped, creating an artful, inviting composition.

Owner Harvey Pollack garnered national media attention in 2007 and again in 2008 by turning off his pumps for twenty-four hours as a protest against oil company profits at the expense of his customers.

WHS Accession 2008/088, photo by Mark Fay

WHS Accession 2008/088, photo by Mark Fay

This modern station features intricate brickwork that references earlier gas station design. Photo by Jim Draeger

32 Milwaukee

4924 West Roosevelt Drive

In 2001, when the former Copeland Service Station reopened as a coffee shop in Milwaukee's Sherman Park neighborhood, the restored building shined as a new chapter in its long and storied history began. Community support, financial assistance, and a creative adaptive reuse had turned what was a dilapidated service station and property into a neighborhood project worth celebrating.

Completed in January 1939 at an estimated cost of three thousand dollars, the Streamlined Moderne-style station reflected the Standard Oil Company's modern image. Walter H. Copeland contracted with Urban F. Peacock and A. C. Runzler to design the station. Peacock, a celebrated Milwaukee architect, was known for his lavish motion picture palaces (including the Oriental Theatre), not gas station designs. Yet, as the Depression years wore on, architects often welcomed projects outside their specialty to stay busy and bring in income.

When Copeland passed away in 1942, his son, Walter Jr., took over until his own death in 1967. Continuing the family business, Wally Copeland, a grandson, ran the station, switching first to Texaco products, then Union 76. Wally sold the station upon his retirement in 1990. A few years later, back taxes and contamination issues almost resulted in its demolition.

Facing a daunting task, Bob and Patrice Olin became the new owners in 2001. They harnessed the energy of local residents, such as Cliff Leppke, looking to revitalize the abandoned property and took advantage of city, county, and state funding, including a brownfield cleanup grant from the Wisconsin Department of Commerce. The project also made use of a new state law that made it easier for cities to return tax-delinquent, contaminated properties to the tax rolls.

The Sherman Perk coffeehouse now serves as a community gathering place. Borrowing from service station design and signage, the new owners even placed the words "coffee" and "cappuccino" over the former service doors that once read "greasing" and "washing." The adaptive reuse of the former Copeland Service Station is a model for the rehabilitation of other derelict stations—an example, as one neighbor notes, of how to live with history.

ca. 1950s.
Courtesy of Bob Olin

WHS Accession 2008/088, photo by Mark Fay

Walter Copeland, the original owner of the Copeland Service Station.
Courtesy of Walter and Sandy Copeland

Bob Olin and his wife, Patrice, at the Sherman Perk coffee shop's grand opening. Courtesy of Bob Olin

Why We Preserve Gas Stations

"**[We] deserve to have monuments** in places that are fun...and remind us of our past, our parents' generation or before—that we deserve the same things. They shouldn't be just walled off and we have to charge admission and want them to go to them. They should be part of our everyday lives. It's what gives us a...rich tapestry in our built environment. And it matters. [People] choose to live in built environments because of the way they look or the way they think they will look in the future. And this neighborhood is no different from any other. This service station's no different than that." —*Cliff Leppke, resident of Milwaukee's Sherman Park neighborhood*[1]

Notes

1. Cliff Leppke, interview by David Hestad, Wisconsin Public Television, August 1, 2006.

33 Muskego

S 98 W 12578 State Trunk Highway 36

In 1892, Prussian immigrant John Bosch purchased his neighbor's business interests, which included a general store and blacksmith shop in Durham, now part of Muskego. Bosch and his family probably sold gasoline from a pump out front like many other small-town merchants who supplied early motorists.

In the early 1920s, the Bosches constructed a simple, rectangular brick service garage with a canted corner at a prime location: the intersection of the newly designated State Trunk Highway 36 (which would be permanently surfaced with concrete by 1925) and U.S. Highway 45. Pumps featuring Wadhams products and later Red Crown gasoline faced this corner, in front of the garage's main entrance. Ed Bosch, John's son, owned and operated the garage for nearly fifty years. Early on, he also sold Pontiac and Buick automobiles.

Around 1946, Ed expanded the original structure, adding new service bays, more garage space, and a massive, two-story tower. With its decorative frieze and conical roof making it look like something from the pages of a fairy tale, the tower became the building's focal point; the main entrance was relocated there. Shaped brick parapets with concrete coping were used throughout the facades.

While it is not known why Ed added on the structure shortly after World War II, one can assume it was to attract even more attention to his business at the already visible corner location. Motorists were sure to take a second look at the huge tower.

Ed owned the garage until his death in 1974. Since then, automotive and tire-sales businesses have utilized the corner location and large garages for purposes similar to the building's original intent.

WHS Accession 2008/088, photo by Mark Fay

Red Crown sign.
Northwoods Petroleum Museum, photo by Joel Heiman

34 Genoa City

N1055 Tombeau Road

Summer tourists have long flocked to southeastern Wisconsin's lakes region. South Nippersink, a small community located there in the village of Genoa City, grew as a resort area in the 1920s and blossomed into a summer community shortly thereafter. Nippersink Manor, one resort with a particularly interesting story, was built in 1922 to cater to those from Chicago, sixty miles to the south, seeking summertime recreation and healthful vacations.

Some resorts, such as those in nearby Lake Geneva, often discriminated against Jewish clientele, so Jews from Chicago and elsewhere worked to establish their own getaways. Nippersink was one of the early resort communities Jews could join to enjoy the area. Eventually, it became well known in the Midwest as a Jewish summer resort. Its population expanded, and summer retreats were created, many in the Tudor Cottage style. As Nippersink Manor continued to attract visitors to its golf course and lodgings, a unique gas station was constructed along the main road leading to the resort.

The incorporation of a gas station in a resort colony demonstrates how the automobile changed the nature of vacationing. No longer relying upon railroads to deliver tourists, resorts embraced the auto traveler. Built in early 1920s, the station, with its tower, low rooflines, and decorative half-timbering, complemented the designs of the other resort buildings including the small, individual cottages. Clearly, the architecture was different from the stations that oil companies were erecting in the 1920s—such as the house-and-canopy-style stations—and it aptly revealed the community's interest in catering to visitors and maintaining an appearance of prosperity and good taste. The smart design didn't mean all customers used common sense, though: in 1926, a motorist lit a match to see how much gas was in his tank and started a memorable fire that luckily was extinguished without threatening the new station.

WHS Accession 2008/088, photo by Mark Fay

While comedians, musicians, and big bands no longer make their way to Nippersink to entertain Jewish vacationers, the resort is still in operation. Now part of what's known as the Nippersink Golf Course and Resort, the former station is used as a workshop.

WHS Accession 2008/088, photo by Mark Fay

35 Oshkosh

420 Division Street

Since the late 1910s, there has been a filling station at this spot just behind the main warehouse building of Thompson Oil and Supply, a firm that sold factory supplies, such as belting and pulleys, and later offered paints, varnishes, and, eventually, gasoline. The small canopied structure changed hands when Thompson was bought out by Cook and Brown Lime and Coal, an old Oshkosh company that eventually operated five gas stations in the city.

In 1934, Cook and Brown knocked down most of the old station, replacing it with a super-service station with Art Deco stylings meant to represent progress and the company's success to its customers. Furthermore, the station was a vast improvement as it had a much more functional and efficient design. When the station formally opened, the company announced that "Now local motorists find our automobile service at our new Light Street Station as complete in its scope as a Super-Market."[9]

An opening-day advertisement boasted that the station's attendants received "thorough training in Scientific Lubrication." The same newspaper ad also sought to assure customers that "When you drive out of our new Station, you can do so knowing that your car will give you longer life and more miles of pleasant, satisfactory performance."[10]

The bold, simple forms of the 1930s stations were, in part, experiments in making the buildings easier to read from passing automobiles. The Oshkosh station's striking modern design featured a lower-roofed operator's office and two service bays that stood higher. Constructed of a cream-colored brick, the vertical lines were embellished with blue glazed brick, likely meant to match the main color of the Dixie Oil and Gasoline product line the station carried.

The station's functional design and service bays served its first owners well until the late 1950s, when Cook and Brown sold the station to Russ Cook and Joe Stravelers. They opened J&R Service and sold Standard Oil products; transmission work was their specialty. When J&R outgrew the space, the owners built a new service garage a few blocks away. These days, lawn mowers and snow blowers are repaired and sold from the former station.

WHS Accession 2008/088, photo by Mark Fay

WHS Accession 2008/088, photo by Mark Fay

Gas pump globe.
Northwoods Petroleum Museum, photo by Joel Heiman

36 Pulaski

159 Pulaski Street

Enterprising businessman Vincent Zielinski built this little house-style canopied station in 1925 in the small town of Pulaski. He also owned and operated a tavern and a ballroom nearby.

The Pulaski Service Station, as it was originally known, featured a hip-roof canopy. The overhang was ringed with lights; the three pumps it sheltered offered Sinclair gasoline. The base of the building was brick and the top half stucco, its office portion well lit thanks to several windows. Located on the prominent corner lot at Main and Pulaski streets, the station was set at a forty-five-degree angle to catch travelers from both streets. The lot was decorated with an outline of white painted rocks, plantings, and a public drinking fountain.

After Zielinski and his wife, Josephine, died, their daughter Agnes continued to run all three businesses and remained a lifelong resident of Pulaski. Leonard Mroczynski was the last person to operate the gas station, which closed when Agnes passed away in 1989.

Tony Hiermonczak now owns the station, as well as Zielinski's Ballroom and Tavern. The structure has been adapted for reuse and now serves as an office for the Pulaski Chamber of Commerce.

Courtesy of Tony Hiermonczak

WHS Accession 2008/088, photo by Mark Fay

37 Stoughton

480 East Main Street

This small, rectangular station was built in Stoughton around 1939–1940. Despite having a string of owners ever since, the structure has changed little.

The designer employed a long band of header bricks in a pattern mirroring the curving parapet at the roofline. The sleek curve—which creates a sense of movement and modernity in the otherwise practical box-type design—terminates just above the small office space in a commonly used 1930s device to differentiate the two parts of the building and call attention to the entrance. Checkerboard-patterned brickwork below the front windows flanking the main entrance contributed a unique element to the station's overall aesthetics.

The two service bays, with their large, multi-pane windows on the side wall, were used for washing, doing repairs, and greasing. The station stopped pumping gas years ago. It has since been used off and on to house a muffler shop and, most recently, a used-car dealership.

WHS Accession 2008/088, photo by Mark Fay

38 Waterford—Wadhams

28407 North Lake Drive

In the late 1880s, August Schmidt settled near the crossroads of two country roads in the small community of Tichigan Corners in the town of Waterford and opened a blacksmithing business. Decades later, it was a logical extension for those in transportation-related businesses—blacksmiths and those who built and repaired carriages—to take on new work related to automobiles. And so, in 1911, August's son, Fred, installed a gas pump out front to serve a noticeable increase in automobile traffic on Big Bend Road (State Trunk Highway 64 today) and in the Racine County resort area.

Fred began selling Wadhams gasoline in 1922 and continued to prosper—so much so that he arranged to have a new service station constructed in place of the blacksmith shop in 1934.

The station, designed by Hugo C. Haeuser, who became the official architect for Wadhams Oil, incorporated characteristics of the Tudor Revival style, including decorative half-timbering. As if the bright red, metal-tile roof was not eye-catching enough, Haeuser added a two-story multisided tower topped with an arrow-shaped weather vane as the main entrance. The design was a marketing device in the mold of the company's earlier exotic, pagoda-inspired stations and built upon the recognizable red roof that symbolized the Wadhams stations. The house-style station, sheathed with brick and stucco, also included two service bays with multi-pane doors.

Shortly after the station was built, the Wadhams newsletter *W-Reminder* included before-and-after photographs of it, noting that "the attractive new station shows, too, how Fred is keeping pace with the times and building a station that is both convenient and pleasing to the eye."[11] Fred was so taken with the design and appearance of his service station that he asked the Milwaukee architect to design his house, also located in Tichigan Corners.

Melvin Grebe, Fred's son-in-law, took over the business in 1946. More than seventy years after it was constructed, the station, now known as the Wadhams Tower Garage, still pumps gas. Fred's grandchildren, Mark and Dona Grebe, operated Hometown Oil Company and a gas station and convenience store out of the building until 2007.

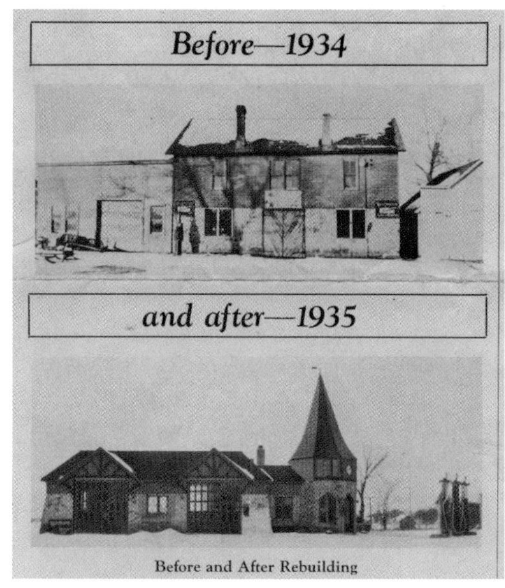

***W-Reminder*, March 1934**

WHS Accession 2008/088, photo by Mark Fay

Fred Schmidt Sr. and Frederick Schmidt Jr., ca. 1940. Courtesy of Mark and Dona Grebe

39 Waterford—Phillips

100 South Jefferson Street

Uncle Harry's Frozen Custard at the corner of Jefferson and Main streets in Waterford is housed in a quaint, cottage-style building that seems as though it was built just for this type of business. The structure, however, started out in 1935 as a Phillips 66 service station.

The domestic and homey station was built by Roy E. Lewis and was, according to the local newspaper, "indeed a beautiful structure."[12] The stucco exterior of the Tudor Revival–style building featured an arch above the entrance, a bay window, and a steeply pitched metal tile roof. A chimney added to the domestic feel and design of the station, which resembled Pure Oil Company's successful English Cottage design.

Lewis's station also promoted its servicing options, including greasing, oiling, and washing. Aiming to impress customers with a sense of progress, Lewis incorporated new technology: gas pumps that automatically registered the amount of gasoline pumped and the price. This in turn improved customer service because patrons could see they were getting the amount of gas they were paying for, which, Lewis hoped, enticed them to return.

Less than two years after it was built, the station was leased by Al Lotsch, who had another station across the street. He renamed this small station Al's Sinclair Service Station; it later became known as Gary's White Flash gas station. The current business began in July 1985 when Harry Dembrowski began serving ice cream, soup, and other specialties out of his gas station. Several owners later, the gas pumps might be gone, but happy customers come back again and again for full-service ice cream and frozen custard.

Northwoods Petroleum Museum, photo by Joel Heiman

WHS Accession 2008/088, photo by Mark Fay

YOU START FASTER

LESS than 2 seconds is the usual starting time of Skelly Tailor-Made Aromax gasoline — even when temperatures drop to zero. Take time for an extra cup of coffee these cold mornings. You won't be "stalled" and late to work—with Skelly Aromax in the tank. Start faster. Warm-up faster. Get extra mileage.

ONLY SKELLY TAILOR-MAKES GASOLINE FOR EACH COMMUNITY

SKELLY originated the tailor-making of gasoline to fit the weather. Still, today, only one gasoline is Tailor-Made for each community. That gasoline is Skelly Aromax. You can buy it only at the sign of the Skelly Diamond.

VIRGIN GASOLINE ADDED TO REFINERY GASOLINE

VIRGIN gasoline is a volatile, high octane, stabilized product—the cleanest, fastest-starting gasoline known. At 24 tailoring points, Skelly adds varying amounts (up to 38%) of Virgin to refinery gasoline, tailoring Aromax for your weather. Try a faster, tailor-made start tomorrow. Drive in where you see the Skelly Tailor.

© 1936, Skelly Oil Co. 613A

Tailor-Made to Fit Your Weather

AROMAX

SKELLY AROMAX

AL'S SERVICE STATION

"SERVICE AS YOU LIKE IT"

WATERFORD — WISCONSIN

Waterford Post, March 4, 1937

40 Watertown

501 South Third Street

It's hard to imagine the opening of a new filling station as a cause for community celebration. But when this little station opened in Watertown on July 30, 1927, the public was invited to inspect the town's newest station and its modern conveniences. Visitors to Fred Pfeifer's station were entitled to one-half gallon of Opaline Motor Oil with a purchase of five gallons of Sinclair gasoline.

Located at the corner of Third and Spring streets, the multicolored brick station featured a steep, side-facing gambrel roof with a clock set into a dormer above the entrance. The building included an office, a ladies' restroom, and a service bay with the station's second gambrel roof, this one over a multi-pane door. The station had a new drain pit—an improvement over the outdated and dangerous rack cars had been driven up onto for oil changes—and also handled greasing, tire repairs, and other light service. A bell in the new automatic pumps rang every time a gallon was pumped into the tank. This neat gimmick reassured customers that the gas was indeed flowing as they saw the total sale price rising.

By 1930, the station was known as Risty's Filling Station. Later purchased by Arnold Karberg, it operated as Karberg's Service Station for forty years. Several businesses, including an auto-detailing shop and an antiques store, have taken up residence there since the mid-1980s, but none have been as successful or active as the early filling station.

ANNOUNCING
The Opening of
SINCLAIR
SERVICE
STATION
Third and Spring Streets
Saturday, July 30th
FREE! ½ GALLON FREE!
SINCLAIR OPALINE MOTOR OIL
"Fits the Degree of Wear"
With each purchase of 5 gallons or more of
SINCLAIR GASOLINE
"Full of Eager Power"
FRED W. PFEIFER
PROPRIETOR

Watertown Daily News, July 29, 1927

WHS Accession 2008/088, photo by Mark Fay

41 West Allis

1647 South Seventy-sixth Street

This small Wadhams station in West Allis is one of a handful of the company's signature pagoda stations still standing. (Another example—a larger, more elaborate station, complete with a multistory pagoda—is in Cedarburg. See page 90.) When it was built in 1927, there were more than thirty Wadhams stations in the greater Milwaukee area and more than one hundred in the Midwest.

The Milwaukee-based Wadhams Oil and Grease Company sought to differentiate its filling stations from the growing number of competitors. Alexander C. Eschweiler, a noted Milwaukee architect of period-revival buildings, designed the Wadhams pagoda prototype. The exotic styling, with the steeply pitched, eye-grabbing red roof and upturned eaves, attracted the attention of motorists and other retailers. This innovation—an effort to tie architecture to corporate image—was quickly adopted by other gas retailers and is referred to as "place-product-packaging" by roadside scholars.

Built at the cost of forty-five hundred dollars, this Wadhams station had a simple brick base and large, multi-pane windows that provided space for product displays and good views of the pumps. Stained-glass windows under each gable featured a red "W" lit from behind.

Frank Seneca was associated with this station for many years. He leased and later owned it for more than four decades, offering prompt service and a sense of community. High school students stopped in for candy and to listen to Brewers games. One former West Allis resident fondly recalled how, when her dad needed gas, all of the kids piled into the car so they could go to the pagoda.

Unable to compete with self-service stations, Seneca closed the station and retired in 1978. Recognizing the building as one of the area's few remaining pagoda stations, the city of West Allis renovated and refurbished it after purchasing the station from Seneca. A small museum of Wadhams petroliana and historic images was completed in 2000. The station was added to the National Register of Historic Places in 2004.

Frank Seneca, ca. 1970s, in front of his station, which is now a petroliana museum.
Courtesy of West Allis Historical Society

WHS Accession 2008/088, photo by Mark Fay

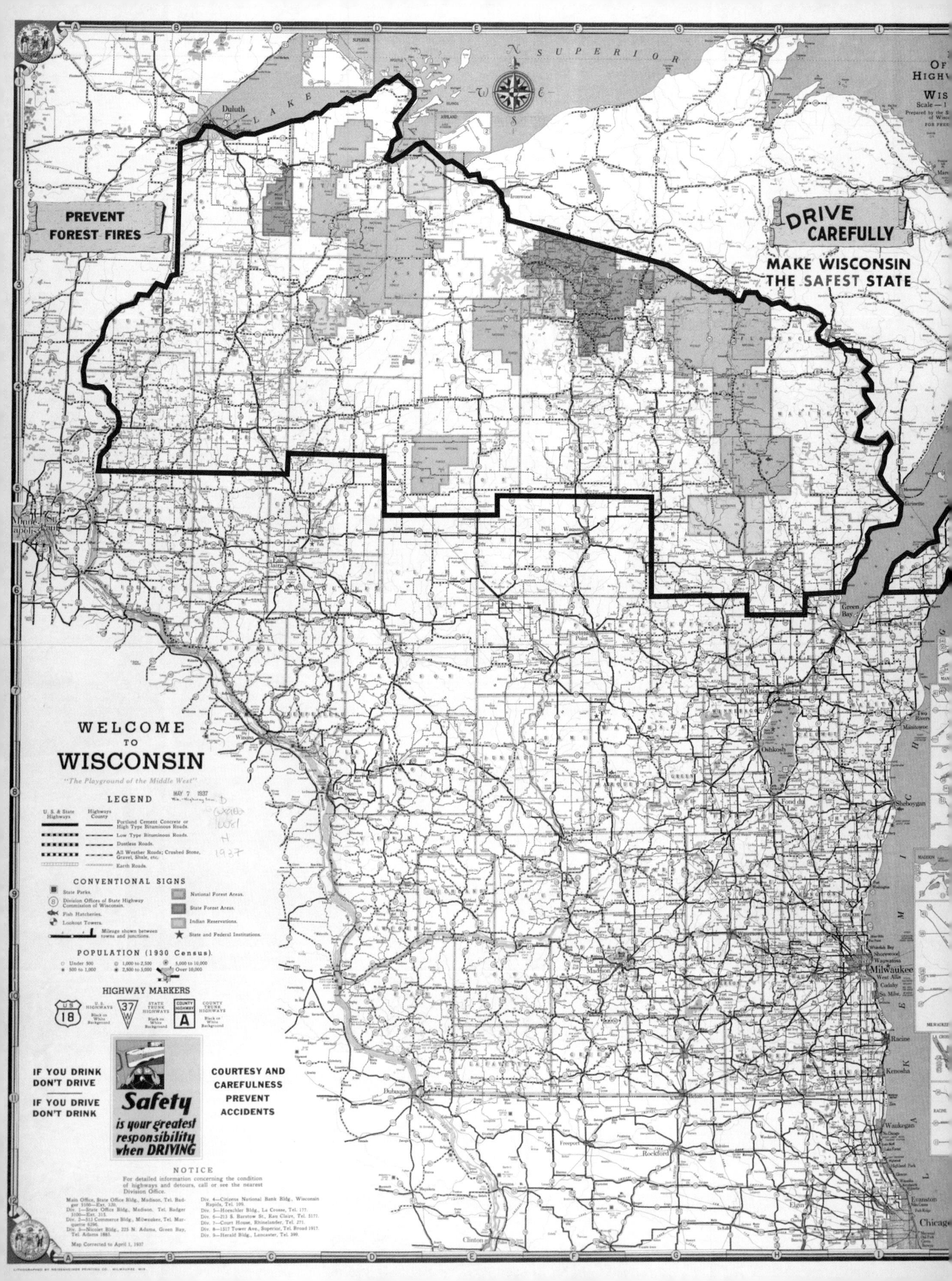
LAKE SUPERIOR
Duluth
Ironwood
PREVENT FOREST FIRES
DRIVE CAREFULLY
MAKE WISCONSIN THE SAFEST STATE
Marinette
Green Bay
Wausau
Eau Claire
Stevens Point
Appleton
Oshkosh
Two Rivers
Manitowoc
Sheboygan
Fond du Lac
La Crosse
Winona
Madison
Milwaukee
Whitefish Bay
Shorewood
Wauwatosa
West Allis
Cudahy
So. Milw.
Racine
Kenosha
Waukegan
Evanston
Chicago
Dubuque
Freeport
Rockford
Elgin
Clinton
WELCOME TO WISCONSIN
"The Playground of the Middle West"
LEGEND
MAY 7 1937
U. S. & State Highways
Highways County
Portland Cement Concrete or High Type Bituminous Roads.
Low Type Bituminous Roads.
Dustless Roads.
All Weather Roads; Crushed Stone, Gravel, Shale, etc.
Earth Roads.
CONVENTIONAL SIGNS
State Parks.
Division Offices of State Highway Commission of Wisconsin.
Fish Hatcheries.
Lookout Towers.
Mileage shown between towns and junctions.
National Forest Areas.
State Forest Areas.
Indian Reservations.
State and Federal Institutions.
POPULATION (1930 Census).
Under 500
500 to 1,000
1,000 to 2,500
2,500 to 5,000
5,000 to 10,000
Over 10,000
HIGHWAY MARKERS
US 18
U. S. HIGHWAYS
Black on White Background
37 W
STATE TRUNK HIGHWAYS
Black on White Background
COUNTY HIGHWAY A
COUNTY TRUNK HIGHWAYS
Black on White Background
IF YOU DRINK DON'T DRIVE
IF YOU DRIVE DON'T DRINK
Safety is your greatest responsibility when DRIVING
COURTESY AND CAREFULNESS PREVENT ACCIDENTS
NOTICE
For detailed information concerning the condition of highways and detours, call or see the nearest Division Office.
Main Office, State Office Bldg., Madison, Tel. Badger 5100—Ext. 120.
Div. 1—State Office Bldg., Madison. Tel. Badger 5100—Ext. 315.
Div. 2—513 Commerce Bldg., Milwaukee, Tel. Marquette 6296.
Div. 3—Nicolet Bldg., 225 N. Adams, Green Bay, Tel. Adams 1883.
Div. 4—Citizens National Bank Bldg., Wisconsin Rapids, Tel. 109.
Div. 5—Hoeschler Bldg., La Crosse, Tel. 177.
Div. 6—213 S. Barstow St., Eau Claire, Tel. 5171.
Div. 7—Court House, Rhinelander, Tel. 271.
Div. 8—1517 Tower Ave., Superior, Tel. Broad 1917.
Div. 9—Herald Bldg., Lancaster, Tel. 399.
Map Corrected to April 1, 1937

NORTH

42 Ashland

522 East Lake Shore Drive

When the East End Co-op Service Station opened at the corner of Sixth Avenue and East Front Street (East Lake Shore Drive today) in 1940, the owners announced, "Our new, modern equipment makes it possible to give your car the most complete one-stop service."[13]

This appeal to service and modernity was also reflected in the design of the station. Owned and constructed by the A&B Cooperative Association, the concrete block structure featured an operator's office with an entrance on the canted corner. Large multi-pane windows provided a clear view of vehicles approaching the pumps. Originally, there were two service bays with concrete pilasters similar to the taller ones on the building's corners. A single band of block running parallel to the roofline added to the station's Art Deco–influenced design.

The station became a family-owned enterprise in 1949 when Ken Arbuckle and his wife purchased it, renaming it Ken's Mobil. The Arbuckles' son, also named Ken, has continued to operate the business. He added a third service bay in 1991 that nicely matched the building's overall design. The business became a Midas franchise in 1992 and, since the underground tanks were updated in 2002, the station still pumps gas.

Announcement
Saturday, August 24
Will Mark the Opening of Your New
East End Co-op Service Station
SIXTH AVENUE EAST & FRONT STREET
Our new, modern equipment makes it possible to give your car the most complete one-stop service.
LET US SERVE YOU THIS NEW Modern Cooperative Way With Better Co-op Merchandise.
A Souvenir Will Be Given Each Customer.
A&B Cooperative Association

Ashland Daily Press, August 22, 1940

WHS Accession 2008/088, photo by Mark Fay

Town of Cassian (Demolished)

7719 U.S. Highway 51

In 1936, Harry Klippel built this gas station, located about six miles south of Hazelhurst in the Town of Cassian, to cater to travelers heading into Wisconsin's North Woods along the newly built Highway 51.

Klippel marketed his log cabin filling station as part of the North Woods experience. He chose a spot where two extremely large white pines flanked the highway. These trees became a symbolic gateway to a North Woods vacation. Through the years, passing motorists honked their horns as they arrived at the place Klippel hoped would signal to tourists that their vacation had already begun and lure them to stop in. Even in recent years, after one of the pines had fallen, travelers were still beeping as they drove by.

Klippel's design for the rustic station was similar to other early house-style stations constructed during the period. The main entrance was centered between two windows, and the roof featured a center gable. A small side door led to a restroom. Klippel lived in a log house next door. He also built a small string of log motel cabins just south of the station and donated land across the highway for a women's club building, also constructed of logs.

Klippel operated the station until 1950; it then changed hands several times. In addition to selling gas, one owner, Walter Slottke, opened a six-stool bar, named Wally and Vera's, in this tiny building. Gas was no longer sold after the mid-1970s, but a bar continued to offer refreshments to local residents and travelers along the highway until the late 1980s. Sadly, this station was recently demolished by the current owner, who, ironically, built a modern, rustic-style building from which to sell North Woods decor.

This log cabin–inspired station, as seen in this 1938 postcard, was designed to welcome tourists to the North Woods. WHi Image ID 58454

Photo by Jim Draeger

Heafford Junction

1972 County Highway L

When Phil Kilinski built this unique Dutch Mill gas station six miles north of Tomahawk, he created a whimsical attraction that successfully drew speeding post–World War II vacationers off what was then U.S. Highway 51.

Constructed in the mid-1940s, the two-and-a-half-story windmill structure had six spinning blades and housed a gas station with three pumps out front that sold Sinclair gasoline. Phil's son, also named Phil, can remember nailing the siding on the structure and helping build it. Window boxes brimming with blossoms added a picturesque quality. Inside, the station sold items for North Woods adventures, such as bait and tackle, and later offered boat rentals in addition to its legendary foot-long hot dogs.

Kilinski built the unique station near the entrance to his successful Phil's Lake Nokomis Resort. The attention-grabbing windmill drew travelers off the road, making them potential customers of the more discreetly placed resort complex.

The gas station venture was short lived. But visitors continued coming, first when the building was converted to a burger joint and, from 1954 until 1963, when another proprietor, a Mrs. Magnus, added more window boxes and sold homemade candies, hand-dipped chocolates, and gifts.

The windmill structure continues to attract travelers, not for gasoline or bait, but for ice cream. The Windmill Ice Cream Shoppe has been in business in the former filling station since the early 1990s.

Courtesy of Russell Berg

WHS Accession 2008/088, photo by Mark Fay

WHS Accession 2008/088, photo by Mark Fay

45 Kennan

W10503 Highway 8

In 1927, Rudy Kuchlenz built this clapboard-sided building at the crossroads of U.S. Highway 8 and County Highway J in the village of Kennan. The commercial building featured a false facade and large front windows, and it housed a small store. The canopy, also with a false-front parapet design, protected Kuchlenz and other attendants from inclement weather while they worked the three pumps, each topped with a Standard Oil crown globe. Kuchlenz also operated a Ford dealership at this location and serviced automobiles in the attached garages.

The station and small store served as a meeting place for residents from the surrounding areas. Having the store and gasoline conveniently at the same location made Kuchlenz's business popular. Kuchlenz's daughter, Elaine Reisner, recalled that it was often busy from five o'clock in the morning until ten o'clock in the evening. With his family housed in the quarters above the station, Kuchlenz operated the business along with his wife, Edith. The long hours made living in the same building an efficient and sound investment, one that was common in many commercial downtown locations where owners lived above their stores. The building is no longer used for commercial purposes.

Late 1940s.
Courtesy of Elaine Reisner

WHS Accession 2008/088, photo by Mark Fay

Elaine Reisner, Rudy Kuchlenz's daughter "filling up" her tricycle, ca. 1935. "Yep: Self-service," she recalls. "Every time I look at this it's as if I'm right there—the cracks in the sidewalk, the garage 'smells.'"
Courtesy of Elaine Reisner

46 Town of Maple Valley

9932 County Trunk Highway M

While growing up in the 1940s, Robert Broetzman hung out at his father's garage, just east of this little station. As a helpful assistant, Broetzman hand-cranked each gallon of gas for his father's customers up into the ten-gallon glass containers of the visible pump. Later in life, Broetzman began to collect pumps, signs, and other petroliana that serve as a reminder of his childhood. He even renovated this little station—a representative of a nearly extinct piece of rural-crossroads architecture.

Located in the small unincorporated community of Hickory Corners in the Town of Maple Valley, this filling station was built in the 1920s by Fred Longard. The building served farmers from the surrounding area and housed a small general store that carried groceries, hardware, supplies, and gasoline. Longard's station had an outdoor pit for oil changes and greasing and sold Sinclair gasoline from pumps situated dangerously close to County Trunk Highway M.

Longard locked up the station in the mid-1930s and moved across the street to a larger building, which housed a new general store with new gas pumps. Longard's daughter Edna and her husband, Bud Lartz, converted the former filling station into a summer cottage.

After buying the old filling station around 1980, Broetzman added the overhang on the side, hung the old advertising signs, and placed a variety of vintage pumps outside for display. Other derelict pumps are arranged in a gas pump cemetery nearby where they "rust in peace." A set of Burma Shave signs—a form of advertising useful back in the days when cars traveled more slowly—helps establish the mood for a nostalgic experience at the former filling station. Broetzman's passion is clearly visible, and many drivers traveling by today crane their necks for a look back—literally and figuratively.

Fred Longard and Pat Parker, who hauled the gas to the station, ca. 1928. Courtesy of Robert and Pat Broetzman

WHS Accession 2008/088, photo by Mark Fay

47 Marinette

1305 Pierce Avenue

Designed to blend into the neighborhood, this appealingly picturesque service station was built about 1933 at the corner of Pierce and Carney avenues in Marinette. Constructed of brick, the station was representative of how the functional requirements of gas retailing could be blended with stylistic features common to Tudor Revival residential structures.

The station featured a large window overlooking the pump island. The roof had flared eaves and decorative half-timbering in the roof's gable peaks and above the main entrance. Multi-pane windows throughout helped brighten the sales office and service garage. The service bay, which was possibly added later, had a bracketed cornice designed to imitate the rhythm of the half-timbered gable ends. Small buttresses with stone caps flanked the entrance and the arched walkway leading to the women's restroom discreetly situated around the side of the building. This attention to detail—a wing wall with its arched entry—created a garden court–like feeling to the space. The added expense of this superfluous element indicated the owner's sensitivity to women as a potential consumer market.

1985.
Historic Preservation Files, Wisconsin Historical Society

The house-style station operated as one of Harry Berg's service stations and, according to a June 6, 1933, advertisement in the *Marinette Eagle Star,* sold Barnsdall's Golden Colored Gasoline for 9.4 cents a gallon. In the late 1940s, it was known as Pete's Skelly service station. When Clem Heil owned and operated the station throughout the 1960 and 1970s, it epitomized the idea of the community gathering place. According to neighbors, Heil and his station were an important part of the neighborhood. He employed young neighborhood boys and relatives, fixed and filled up children's bike tires, and maintained charge accounts for scores of customers often known on a first-name basis. The station later became a Mobil station. It eventually housed a Domino's Pizza shop and, most recently, a dry-cleaning business.

WHS Accession 2008/088, photo by Mark Fay

Northwoods Petroleum Museum, photo by Joel Heiman

48 Milltown

118 Highway 35

This unique station in Milltown visually illustrates its ongoing changes and success over time as it responded to competition and evolving needs that typify the gas-retailing business.

Built sometime in the mid-1930s, this station originally sold Standard Oil products. Based on the visual clues, the station may have begun as a simple filling station and possibly featured a canopy over the pump island. The independent Erickson Company purchased the station in 1939, adding it to the company's large regional chain.

It's possible that the station was remodeled at this time in the Streamlined Moderne style, reflecting a popular fad to mimic the aerodynamic lines of ocean liners and airplanes in a variety of consumer goods from pencil sharpeners to plumbing fixtures. Streamlining became an icon of modernity and was enthusiastically adopted in products associated with speed, such as gas stations. Stylistic elements included this station's rounded corner, flat roof, two horizontal beltcourses (now painted red), and smooth, sleek surface of stucco. A large window sat on each side of the entrance, while a porthole window (borrowed from ocean liner design) decorated the rounded end. It's likely the two service bays were added after the original construction; the large vertical pylon visually connected the two spaces.

As the gas-retailing business changed over time, the Erickson Company—known for its super-cut-rate gas specials—dropped auto service and built more modern stations. The company focused on high-volume locations and utilized all-glass facades, slanted columns supporting an overhang topped with its large sign, and assertive overhead lighting above the pumps to attract motorists in the day and night.

This station closed in the mid-1950s when Erickson (now known as Holiday) built a new station across the street. The old station eventually did duty as a Ford dealership, a repair shop, and, most recently, a construction business.

WHS Accession 2008/088, photo by Mark Fay

49 Minocqua

329 Front Street

According to the *Minocqua Times*, work began on this yellow-glazed brick station in late 1931. Based on plans from the Texas Oil Company, the station's design featured segmental brick arches over the two service bay doors and windows and a Texaco clock inset above the entrance. The facade also included two beltcourses of green glazed brick. Green brick geometric patterns between all of the openings were another design element.

William Siebel operated the station during its early years and later owned it with his wife, Martha. The station served countless North Woods vacationers—reputedly including the Chicago gangster Al Capone. William "Bill" Siebel II, grandson of the early owner, remembers hearing his father, Tony, tell stories of Capone and his associates pulling in for a fill-up.

Tony Siebel's Texaco pin.
Courtesy of William Siebel II

During the 1960s, the station sold Zephyr gas. Following the deaths of the Siebels, the station closed in 1970 and became an auto-detailing business. The former Texaco station is still in the transportation business: Instead of filling up their gas tanks, vacationers can fill up their tires, get bicycle tune-ups, and rent bicycles to pedal around the streets of Minocqua.

The Siebel family outside their standard-design Texaco station.
Courtesy of William Siebel II

WHS Accession 2008/088, photo by Mark Fay

50 Osceola

202 North Cascade Street

This Art Moderne service station undoubtedly grabbed the attention of postwar motorists with its dramatically curved facade. Even now, the station—situated within Osceola's Commercial Historic District, which is on the National Register of Historic Places—contrasts sharply with the turn-of-the-last-century designs of its downtown neighbors.

Arthur Andren built this station on North Cascade Street in 1947 using standardized building plans provided by the Socony-Vacuum Oil Company. New York architect Frederick Frost designed the prototype for the oil company, incorporating its corporate symbol—the oil drum—as a focal point. The dramatic design included showroom windows, two service bays, and wing walls flanking each side of the corner lot. In addition to the building's design, the company (later known as Mobil) relied on the station's colors, signage, and red Pegasus logo to establish its corporate identity. Roadside buffs consider the Mobil drum station one of the most iconic designs of the midcentury. Its sleek, simple lines evoked the fluid forms of period automobiles.

The station was operated by Martin Kraska in the 1950s. In addition to tune-ups, brakes, tires, greasing, and washing, Kraska's Mobil Service sold portable air conditioners for cars and homes and even carried minnows. The station later became a Skelly station before closing in the 1980s. It has since been remodeled. Its former salesroom and service bays have become a law office.

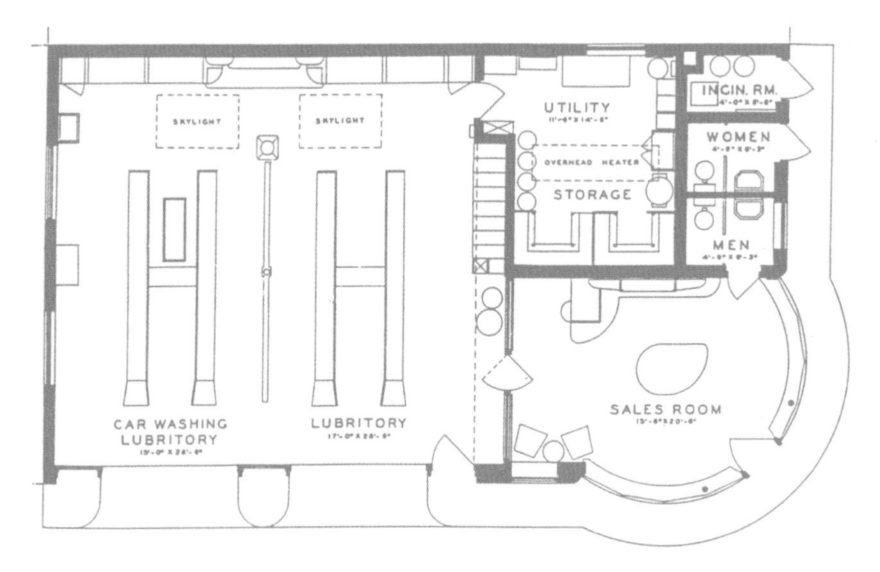

Floor plan of the basic Socony-Vacuum Oil Company drum-style station, a variation on the box-type design. Mobil Corporate Archives

WHS Accession 2008/088, photo by Mark Fay

ca. 1958.
1958 Osceola Phone Directory

51 Pence

6850 West Highway 77

By the time Gus Savera built his service garage along Highway 77, he was already a veteran mechanic.

Located west of Hurley in the small town of Pence, the service garage was constructed of cinder blocks and featured bright blue trim. At the center of the stepped-parapet, false-front facade built in the mid-1940s was a big red "S" for "Savera."

Savera's early love for automobiles led him to a Ford Motor School in Detroit, where he trained as a mechanic. Afterward, he worked at several garages in Ironwood, Michigan, and did repair jobs in the evenings at his garage across the border in Pence. Gas pumps were installed in 1956, when Savera started his business full-time at this location. He did the repairs and pumped gas while his wife, Chris, helped with the bookkeeping.

Savera's auto business continued until 1982, when he reduced the operation to mainly gas sales, often just a few dollars' worth per day. Savera's son, Ray, recalling his dad's experience in those later years, said, "Customers would drop by and buy two dollars' worth of gas and then spend a half hour gabbing. He loved it!"

Over the years, Savera trained and employed Bob Olson, who purchased the property after Savera's death in 2000. As a show of his respect and affection, Olson, who continued the auto-repair business, still includes Gus's name on the list of mechanics on duty.

Chris and Gus Savera, 1983.
Courtesy of Ray Savera

WHS Accession 2008/088, photo by Mark Fay

Courtesy of Ray Savera

52 Sturgeon Bay

253 Michigan Street

A good location is imperative to the success of any gas station. Since the 1930s, this busy corner in Sturgeon Bay has been the site of a succession of gas stations that have continually evolved to reflect changes in the gas-retailing industry.

Standard Oil Company, which owned a two-bay, box-type station here from the 1940s to 1960s, leased out the station to a series of operators, most of whom stayed a short time. The station's shiny porcelain-enamel facade attracted the attention of countless Door County visitors, who stopped to fill their tanks on their way up the peninsula.

In 1971, the pressure to make room for more pumps forced the owners to demolish the existing building and locate a new, larger station near the back of the sizable corner lot. Functionally, the station was simply a bigger box-type design, now with three service bays; its Colonial-style exterior was a response to the growing popularity of Colonial- and ranch-style designs in the 1960s and 1970s. Perched on the edge of the transition to self-service, the station offered one pump island devoted to full-service and two islands with self-service. The owners clearly still relied heavily on vehicle-service revenues in the two service bays, but a car wash occupied the third bay. This arrangement lasted nearly two decades, before change again transformed the site.

In the late-1980s, Charles Wiegand (who had previously leased the site in the 1950s), his wife, Ada, and four sons, Dan, Dale, Dave, and Duane, leased the station before purchasing it outright a few years later. The family's success with a large convenience store station in Algoma convinced them to apply the same business model to this Sturgeon Bay location. So the Colonial-style station got another makeover as a convenience store. The service bays were replaced with aisles of convenience foods, milk, beverages, and other impulse purchases.

The change made sense for the family business and for its customers. During this period, large chains of specialized auto-repair shops, such as brake and muffler shops, were making the vehicle-service business more competitive. Self-service gasoline also dominated the industry. The Wiegands converted the full-service island to self-service about this time, investing in a massive forty-five-by-forty-eight-foot canopy over the pump islands. Steel King in Waupun built the canopy, which was installed to protect customers from the changeable Door County weather. After many years at this location, the Wiegand family decided to get out of the gas-retailing business and sold the station in 2004.

WHS Accession 2008/088, photo by Mark Fay

A box-type station stood on this site from the 1940s to 1960s. **Courtesy of Duane Wiegand**

Attendants in front of the station's pumps, topped with Standard Oil glass globes, ca. 1960s. **Courtesy of Duane Wiegand**

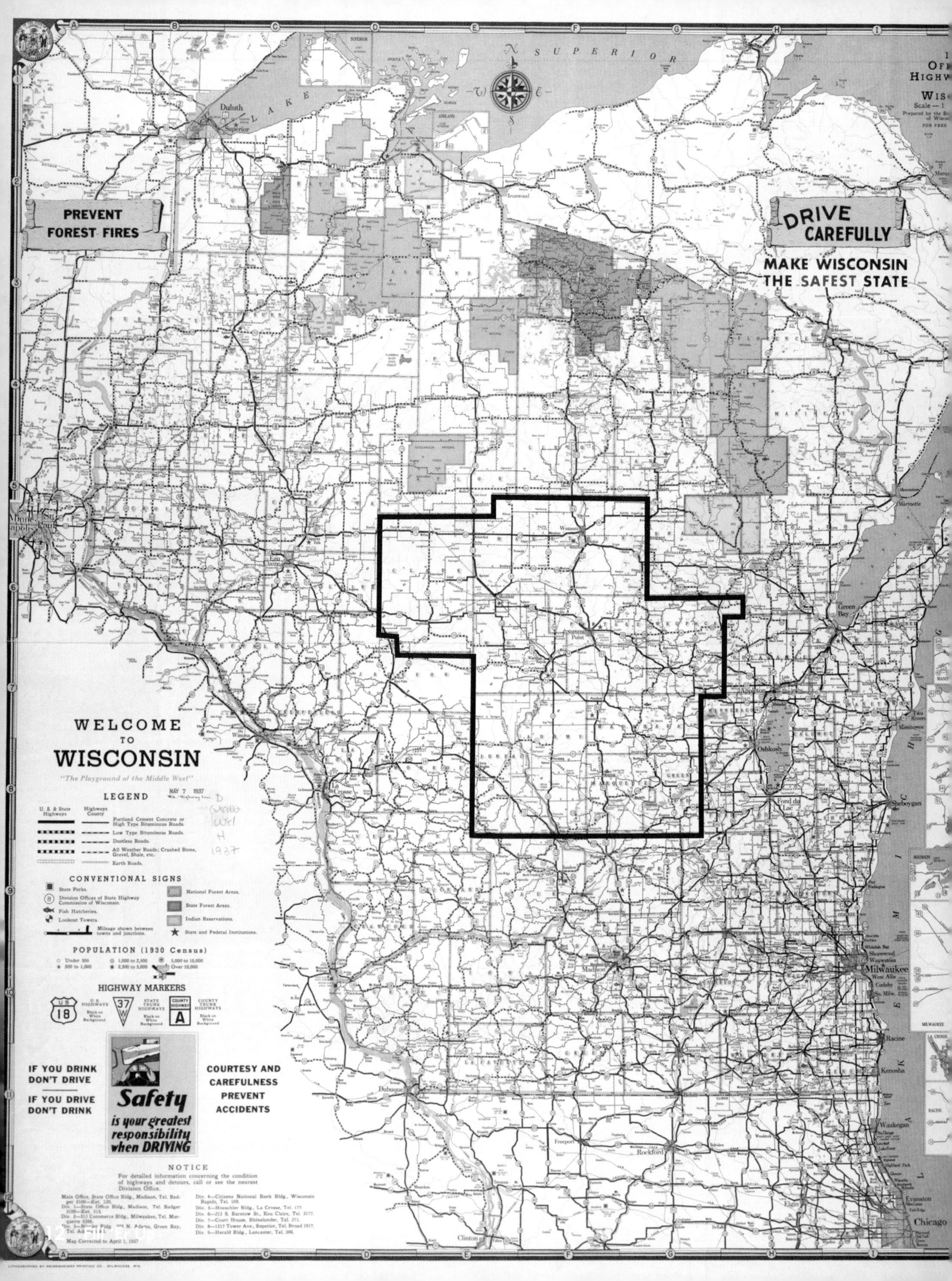
LAKE SUPERIOR
Duluth
Superior
Ironwood
Wausau
Green Bay
Oshkosh
Fond du Lac
Sheboygan
Milwaukee
Madison
Racine
Kenosha
Waukegan
Chicago
Rockford
Freeport
Dubuque
La Crosse
Winona
Eau Claire
Marinette
PREVENT FOREST FIRES
DRIVE CAREFULLY
MAKE WISCONSIN THE SAFEST STATE
WELCOME TO WISCONSIN
"The Playground of the Middle West"
LEGEND
U. S. & State Highways
Highways County
Portland Cement Concrete or High Type Bituminous Roads.
Low Type Bituminous Roads.
Dustless Roads.
All Weather Roads; Crushed Stone, Gravel, Shale, etc.
Earth Roads.
CONVENTIONAL SIGNS
State Parks.
Division Offices of State Highway Commission of Wisconsin.
Fish Hatcheries.
Lookout Towers.
Mileage shown between towns and junctions.
National Forest Areas.
State Forest Areas.
Indian Reservations.
State and Federal Institutions.
POPULATION (1930 Census)
Under 500
500 to 1,000
1,000 to 2,500
2,500 to 5,000
5,000 to 10,000
Over 10,000
HIGHWAY MARKERS
US 18
U.S. HIGHWAYS Black on White Background
37 W
STATE TRUNK HIGHWAYS Black on White Background
COUNTY HIGHWAY A
COUNTY TRUNK HIGHWAYS Black on White Background
IF YOU DRINK DON'T DRIVE
IF YOU DRIVE DON'T DRINK
Safety is your greatest responsibility when DRIVING
COURTESY AND CAREFULNESS PREVENT ACCIDENTS
NOTICE
For detailed information concerning the condition of highways and detours, call or see the nearest Division Office.
Main Office, State Office Bldg., Madison, Tel. Badger 5100—Ext. 120.
Div. 1—State Office Bldg., Madison, Tel. Badger 5100—Ext. 313.
Div. 2—513 Commerce Bldg., Milwaukee, Tel. Marquette 6396.
Div. 4—Citizens National Bank Bldg., Wisconsin Rapids, Tel. 109.
Div. 5—Hoeschler Bldg., La Crosse, Tel. 177.
Div. 6—213 S. Barstow St., Eau Claire, Tel. 5177.
Div. 7—Court House, Rhinelander, Tel. 271.
Div. 8—1517 Tower Ave., Superior, Tel. Broad 1917.
Div. 9—Herald Bldg., Lancaster, Tel. 399.
Map Corrected to April 1, 1937
MAY 7 1937

CENTRAL

Mobilgas SPECIAL
Mobilgas
Mobilgas SPECIAL
GASOHOL
THIS PUMP
GULF

53 Berlin

224 Ripon Road

Edward and Walter Biegick started with a tire-repair shop in 1918 and went on to operate a service station and large automobile dealership in downtown Berlin. The *Berlin Evening Journal* noted in a 1925 article, "It takes pep, energy, hustle, and service to make a reputation and hold it. Biegick Bros have done both."[14] Their entrepreneurial spirit continued as they acquired a station in Ripon and built this small station.

The early years at the Biegick brothers' station.
Courtesy of Berlin Historical Society

Ornamental concrete blocks designed to look like cut stone were intended to give the humble station a more respectable finish. The little station also had a flower box below the front window and an Adirondack chair for the attendant to lounge in while waiting for customers.

The station was sold in the early 1930s to Walter Jantz, who pumped Shell gasoline and sold Goodyear Tires. He later constructed a single service bay using materials similar to the original. A large sign above the glass-and-wood service door advertised "SHELLUBRICATION." Hubert Weir bought the station from Jantz in the early 1970s and ran it as a Shell station until closing it in 1988. It currently houses a vintage-auto restoration business.

The station as it looked under Walter Jantz's ownership.
Courtesy of Berlin Historical Society

WHS Accession 2008/088, photo by Mark Fay

54 Manawa

301 South Bridge Street

This service station was built in Manawa during the late 1930s as new, more efficient station designs were constructed throughout the state. Yet some owners, like Vilas Topp, still chose older styles for their stations, often with one foot in the past and one in the future.

Topp selected a design that represented a transition between two styles. He clearly sought to capitalize upon the house-style-with-canopy design. He also set his station at the corner of Bridge and Union at an angle to attract motorists from both streets, a placement that worked well for small filling stations. Yet Topp also had his eye on servicing automobiles, and so he included two service bays in the design. In fact, the station's overall shape was similar to the more efficient box-style stations that would dominate the gas-retailing industry for decades to come.

The station was beautifully constructed of multicolored brick, and the metal-clad tile roof visually tied together the filling and service areas. But the site placement was ill suited for the addition of bays: drivers pulling under the canopy would veer out in front of the service bays, increasing chances for delays or, worse, fender benders.

The operator's room was rectangular and larger than those in most early stations. The facade featured an entrance with a display window on each side. The canopy, which was supported by two brick columns, originally covered three Standard gasoline pumps and afforded protection from the elements for one automobile.

Courtesy of Gary and Judy Heise

In 1968, the station was purchased by brothers Gary and Norm Heise from the second owners, George and Al Schuelke. The Heise brothers continued selling gasoline, later switching to Skelly products. They serviced and repaired automobiles until 1992, when the property was sold to Suehs Motors, which performs detailing work in this building and uses it as a car lot.

WHS Accession 2008/088, photo by Mark Fay

55 Waupaca

206 West Fulton Street

In the late 1910s and early 1920s, Gray Czeskleba and his father ran a hardware store in Waupaca from which they likely sold gasoline to early motorists. Czeskleba turned exclusively to gasoline and oil distribution in 1925, and by the time he built this filling station in 1933, he was operating one of the town's most prominent oil and gas businesses.

Czeskleba already owned and operated a bulk plant and two stations when he acquired this corner property at West Fulton and Washington streets, where there had been a wagon and blacksmith shop for many years. Like other entrepreneurs of this period, Czeskleba hoped the same location that had proved profitable during the horse-and-buggy days would be a good bet for the auto trade.

The Tudor Revival–style station opened for business in the summer of 1933. Meant to resemble a small house and provide a welcoming and reassuring atmosphere for customers, the two-story station featured a steeply pitched gable roof with pointed arch openings. The swayback roof also included a gable front above the main entrance, which was balanced by multi-pane windows on each side. The brickwork flared out at each of the four corners, adding to the storybook-like appearance.

Czeskleba died a year after the station was built, but his wife continued to run the company for many years after. The double service bay was a post-1950s addition. The structure has housed real estate businesses, most recently Shambeau & Lyons, since the pumps were removed in the 1970s.

WHS Accession 2008/088, photo by Mark Fay

56 Westfield

627 Main Street

Gas station owners along busy highways continually sought to capture the attention—and dollars—of the steady stream of tourists headed off on vacation each year. Stations themselves were rarely destinations, but retailers worked hard to convince drivers to take a break en route and hoped to pull them off the road. Marketing slogans and building materials, such as logs and rustic siding, were used to evoke a sense of adventure, exoticism, and vacation.

Hoping to transform travelers driving north along old Highway 51 in the mid-1930s into customers, Theo Bertin built this small house-and-canopy station. Located at the corner of Main and Seventh streets in Westfield, the station was touted as the "Gateway to the North."

Bertin borrowed a popular marketing concept aimed at auto tourists. A number of Wisconsin communities claimed to be the "Gateway to the North," such as nearby Portage, which emblazoned the same phrase on the roof ridge of the pavilion in Riverside Park. To the north, Stevens Point claimed to be the "Gateway to the Pineries," cashing in on the distinct change of forest cover from the oaks of southern Wisconsin to the white pines of the North Woods. The notion of a gateway was a powerful psychological incentive for travelers to take a rest and relax, since they had essentially arrived at the start of their getaway.

Bertin constructed the station of brick, topped with a metal-tile roof. The large windows helped light the interior space and provided clear views of approaching motorists. Two tall glass-topped pumps featuring Sinclair products originally sat under the canopy.

Bertin ran the station for the twenty or more years it was open, living in the house next door. When the station closed in the 1950s, the pumps and tanks were removed. The former filling station, which has seen little use since, serves as a ghostly reminder of the early decades of motoring, travel, and our continual fascination with escaping to the North Woods to get away from it all.

WHS Accession 2008/088, photo by Mark Fay

57 Wild Rose

430 Main Street

Motorists in 1928 would have known from the bright red tile roof that this little filling station proudly sold Wadhams gasoline. While the station is quite small, its architectural advertisement was visible many blocks away.

Herman Hanson built the small rectangular brick station before the spring of 1928. The original office area included two large front windows on each side of the main entrance. Although the metal-tile roof featured the distinctive red paint, the shape was less flamboyant than some of the more exotic pagoda-style stations Wadhams built. Currently, the station's brick walls are covered with stucco and painted white.

The service bay and hoist were added sometime in the 1940s and were a definite improvement over the original outdoor pit that was used for oil changes and other services. Yet, according to a former operator, Norman Hoeft, even with the enclosed bay, life was not always easy. Hoeft remembers the time when he had a car on the hoist in winter. There was no heat in the basement, and when the customer came, the hoist would not come down. Despite the efforts of six people hanging from the bumpers, Hoeft had to send the customer home in his car. Two days later, the hoist finally thawed enough to come down.

Hoeft, who rented the station from Hanson for one cent per gallon prior to World War II, left in the 1950s to become an area agent for Standard Oil. After Hanson, Henry Lauritzen owned the station from the early 1950s until it closed in 1978. Most recently, the small building and service bay has housed a motorcycle-repair business.

ca. 1995.
Photo by Jim Draeger

WHS Accession 2008/088, photo by Mark Fay

58 Wisconsin Rapids—Airport Bar-B-Q

329 Front Street

When this structure hosted its grand-opening celebration in 1931, the special was not discounted gasoline or oil but chicken and barbecue sandwiches—and "souvenirs for everyone."

Constructed by local builder Gilbert Sandman for the Radomski family, the multipurpose building housed both a filling station and the Airport Bar-B-Q restaurant. Clad with rustic imitation log siding, the large building included spacious dining rooms, a salesroom, and living quarters for the Radomskis.

William Radomski sold Globe gasoline and Veedol oils from his station just south of Wisconsin Rapids. The canopy out front, which was supported by rough-hewn posts, covered two gas pumps and had space for one automobile.

This station catered to travelers, offering both food and gasoline, in a similar way to the co-branded locations that line the interstates today. More than seventy years ago, the Airport Bar-B-Q foreshadowed the truck stops and the fast-food/gas station combinations of the future.

Terry Wolfe purchased the structure in the early 1970s, using the space to house his realty company. Except for the addition of the large dormers, little has changed on the exterior since the building's construction.

Globe sign.
Northwoods Petroleum Museum, photo by Joel Heiman

WHS Accession 2008/088, photo by Mark Fay

59 Wisconsin Rapids—Sinclair

410 East Grand Avenue

"Come In and Buy, or Just Look Around. Inspect the complete facilities for washing—tire and battery service and our stock of accessory items" proclaimed Carl Miller and Joe Walloch in a grand-opening advertisement.[15] They welcomed future customers to their new station in August 1940 with a great opening special: seven gallons of Pennant gas for one dollar.

The service station was constructed of tile blocks and steel along modern lines. The stylish, streamlined front windows with rounded ends provided a clear view of the pumps and driveways and offered display areas for products. The exterior originally included two bands across the top of the operator's section along with matching bands on the chimney.

The two service bays, which have since been filled in, originally featured two large glass doors, with six-lights-over-five windows. In addition to the banding motif, the words "Greasing" and "Washing" appeared over each of the doors. The highly visible words reminded motorists while their tanks were being filled up with Sinclair gasoline products of the additional services Miller and Walloch offered.

During the late 1950s, this station became known as Charles Liska's Service Station. It remained a Sinclair station until the 1970s, when it sold Shell products. After the tanks were pulled in the 1970s, a series of vacuum and sewing businesses have continually utilized the former service station, making use of its large display windows. As we prepared this book for publication, the current owners of Miller and Walloch's station radically altered the building—squaring off its rounded corner and adding a second floor, leaving the building unrecognizable today.

ca. 1995.
Photo by Jim Draeger

WHS Accession 2008/088, photo by Mark Fay

GRAND OPENING

Here's A Cordial Invitation To Every Motorist In This Vicinity
To Visit Our New Station On Its Formal Opening Day

SATURDAY, AUGUST 31

LOADS OF SUCCESS
is our wish for
Carl Miller & Joe Walloch
upon completion of their Beautiful New SERVICE STATION and MODERN BULK PLANT.

We were glad of the opportunity to furnish Fixtures and other electrical work at both places.

Johnson Electric
121 Third Ave. S. Tel. 67

Our New Station at East Grand and 4th St.

Come In And Buy, or
Just Look Around

Inspect the complete facilities for washing---tire and battery service and our stock of accessory items.

Ready to Serve You
Carl Miller and Joe Walloch

Congratulations—
to
Carl Miller & Joe Walloch
of the
Miller-Walloch Oil Co.
On the Completion of their Beautiful New Service Station.

Daly Lumber & Fuel Co.
COAL—Lumber - Millwork—ICE
Building Materials

It was our pleasure to be selected to furnish
SIGNS
and
NEON TUBING
For the
Miller-Walloch Oil Co.
AND WISH TO OFFER HEARTY CONGRATULATIONS AND BEST WISHES FOR SUCCESS.

A.L. Thomas Signs
Tel. 1842

We Feature These Famous Sinclair Products

Sinclair H-C Gasoline
For performance it has no superior in its price class.

Sinclair Opaline and Sinclair Pennsylvania Motor Oils

Sinclair Lubricants
I apply these lubricants according to a special chart for your car contained in my Sinclair lubrication index. The chart shows your car manufacturer's recommendations. This kind of lubrication helps prevent repairs—makes your car safer and easier to drive.

Sinclair Fuel Oil

WHEN YOU VISIT THE
Miller-Walloch Station
Inspect the
PLUMBING
By
HESS PLBG. CO.
430 E. Grand Ave. Phone 370

We Were
THE ARCHITECTS
For the

Miller and Walloch's grand opening garnered a full-page advertisement.
Wisconsin Rapids Daily Tribune, August 30, 1940

Appendix

Map of Station Locations

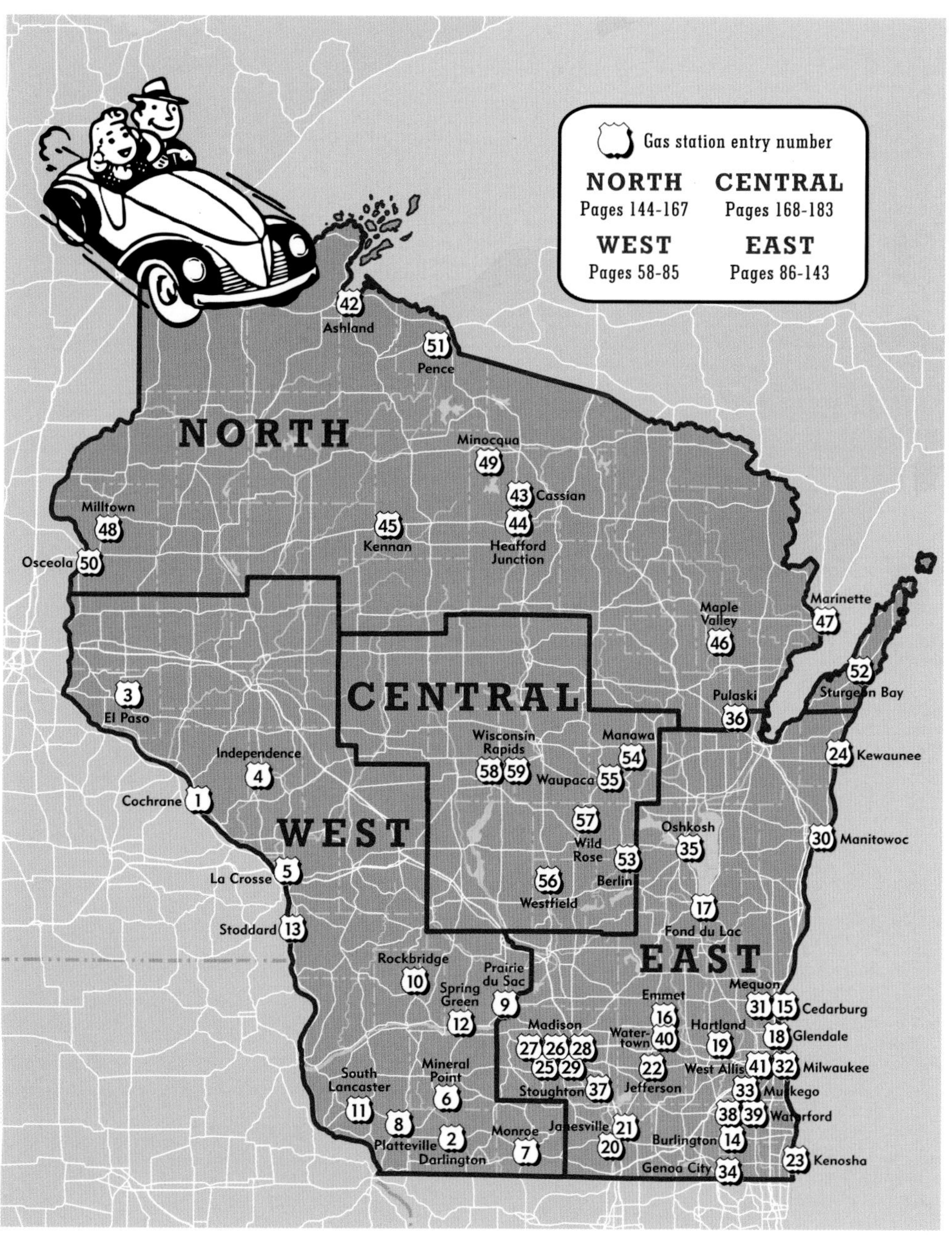

Map by David Michael Miller

Notes

Wisconsin Gas Stations

1. John Kenneth Galbraith, "To My New Friends in the Affluent Society—Greetings," *Life*, March 27, 1970: p. 20.
2. "How Motor Car Grew from Toy to World Industry; Only Seven Autos in First Parade Held in Milwaukee," *Milwaukee Telegram*, August 6, 1922.
3. Untitled newspaper clipping, *Wisconsin State Journal*, November 21, 1900, p. 1b, from O. J. Thompto personal collection.
4. "Denu Starts Oil Business," *Wisconsin State Journal*, September 13, 1904, p. 8c, from O. J. Thompto personal collection.
5. C. A. Crosser, "Curbing the Curb Pump," *American City,* August 1923, p. 55.
6. "Filling Station Owner Relocates Highway," *Watertown Daily News*, June 25, 1927; "Road Didn't Pass His Place, So He Changed the Signs," *Milwaukee Journal*, June 24, 1927.
7. "Through the Windshield," *Wisconsin State Journal*, July 20, 1924.
8. J. F. Kuntz, "Greek Architecture and Gasoline Service Stations," *American City*, August 1922, p. 123.
9. Undated newspaper clipping, *Capital Times*, 1927, from O. J. Thompto personal collection.
10. Alexander Guth, "Small Buildings: The Automobile Service Station," *Architectural Forum* 45:1, July 1926: pp. 33–56.
11. Ibid.
12. Ibid.
13. Carl A. Petersen, design for a service-station booth, U.S. Patent D 77857, issued February 26, 1929.
14. "Bungalow Filling Station at Waupun Attracts Many Passing Tourists," *The Master Builder*, June 1927: p. 7.
15. "Three Hurt as Exploding Gas Demolishes Park Station, Rocks Houses," *Wisconsin State Journal*, June 17, 1933.
16. Correspondence Leo Salkowski to Industrial Commission of Wisconsin, April 1936, Wisconsin Historical Society archival collections, series 2284, box 297.
17. Note to file Industrial Commission of Wisconsin, March 2, 1939, Wisconsin Historical Society archival collections, series 2284, box 213.
18. "Ordinance to Bar Any New Mainstreet Gas Stations," *Stoughton Courier-Hub,* December 6, 1939.
19. Pennco promotional material, 1930, in O. J. Thompto personal collection.
20. *Wadham's Gasoline Station Manual*, undated ca. 1930, from the collections of the Center for American History, University of Texas at Austin.

21. Ibid.

22. Ibid.

23. Ibid.

24. U.S. Department of Labor, Bureau of Labor Statistics, *Wages and Hours of Labor in Gasoline Filling Stations and Motor-Vehicle Repair Garages: 1931*, bulletin no. 578, February 1933.

25. K. Lönberg-Holm, "The Gasoline Filling and Service Station," *Architectural Record* 67:6, June 1930: pp. 561–584.

26. "Planning Techniques for New and Remodeled Buildings," *Architectural Forum*, February 1937: p. 86.

27. "Job at Filling Station Is 'Fun,' Woman Says," *Capital Times*, June 22, 1946.

28. James Grant, "The Arabs' New Oil Squeeze: Dimouts, Slowdowns, Chills," *Time*, November 19, 1973: pp. 88–95.

29. Marvin Reid, "How the Self-Serve Revolution Bred Price Wars and C-Stores," *National Petroleum News*, February 1984: p. 92.

30. Ibid.

31. Dennis McCann, "Forget Self-Serve," *Milwaukee Journal, Wisconsin Magazine* section, March 20, 1988.

32. "Rid Your Neighborhood of Eyesores: City Can Help by Condemning Buildings," George Bulter Aldermanic Newsletter, City of Milwaukee, Winter 1995, p. 5.

59 Historic Stations

1. "New Station Opens," *Darlington Democrat,* June 11, 1931.

2. Advertisement, *La Crosse Tribune and Leader-Press*, October 22, 1937.

3. "Freitag Service Station Opening Is Announced," *Monroe Evening Times*, September 28, 1935.

4. Trachte Portable Steel Garage and Building Catalog (Madison, WI: Trachte Brothers Company, ca. 1927), p. 16.

5. "Hansen Oil Co. New Gas Station," *Burlington Standard Democrat,* March 25, 1927.

6. Advertisement, *Jefferson Banner,* October 8, 1936.

7. "New Wadham's Station Completed," *Kewaunee Enterprise*, August 28, 1931.

8. Advertisement, *Manitowoc Herald News*, August 5, 1927.

9. Advertisement, *Oshkosh Northwestern*, June 6, 1934.

10. Advertisement, *Oshkosh Northwestern*, May 29, 1934.

11. Wadhams Oil Company, *The W-Reminder*, no. 77, March 22, 1934.

12. "New Gas Station Opens in Village," *Waterford Post*, August 1, 1935.

13. Advertisement, *Ashland Daily Press*, August 22, 1940.

14. Ray S. Starks, "Service Spells Success in Motor Firm Operated by Biegick Brothers," *Berlin Evening Journal*, August 3, 1925.

15. Advertisement, *Wisconsin Rapids Daily Tribune*, August 30, 1940.

Index

Page numbers in *italics* refer to illustrations.

Wilton
Kendall
EL. 1012
Mauston
Easton
EL. 1073
Montello
Lemonweir
Oxford
Packwaukee
Packwaukee Jct.
L. Puckaway
Glendale
Elroy
Plainville
Buffalo
Endeavor
Glen Oak
Marquette
Kingston
Trippville
Union Cen.
Lyndon
UPPER DELLS
Big spring
Mt. Tabor
Wonewoc
Briggsv.
Dalton
Hillsboro
Dilly
Wisconsin Dells
Lake Delton
LOWER DELLS
EL. 898
OLD INDIAN AGENCY HOUSE
La Valle
Valton
Reedsburg
Portage
Yuba
Ironton
Pardeeville
Cazenovia
Ableman
Wyocena
Hub City
NATURAL BRIDGE
Limeridge
Baraboo
BLUFFS
Doyles town
Bloom City
Rio
Rock bridge
Hillpoint
Loganville
Hartman
Loyd
N. Freedom
DEVIL'S LAKE
Buckcreek
LaRue
BARABOO
GAME FARM
Otsego
Poynette
Sandusky
Loretta
SAUK
COLUMBIA
Merrimac
N. Leeds
RICHLAND
NATURAL BR.
FREE FERRY
Arlington
Richland Center
Ithaca
Bear Valley
White Mound
Leland
Denzer
Okee
EL. 848
Lodi
Leeds
Keyeser
Prairie du Sac
Basswood
Sextonville
Black Hawk
Morrisonville
Norway Gr.
N. Bristol
Twin Bluffs
Gotham
Plain
Sauk City
Roxbury
DeForest
Spring Green
Dane
Windsor
Sun Prairie
Marx ville
Springfield Cors.
Waunakee
Muscoda
Avoca
Lone Rock
TOWER HILL STATE PARK
Mazomanie
Black Earth
Clyde
Hillside
Arena
Ashton
Mendota
Wyoming
Cross Plains
Lake Mendota
Madison
Pine Bluff
Middleton
L. Monona
Cottage Gr.
Highland
Standart
Hyde
EL. 1226
U. S. FOREST PROD. LABORATORY
IOWA
Barneveld
Mt. Horeb
Kievenville
Ridgeway
Blue Mounds
Verona
L. Waubesa
STATE FISH HATCHERY
Mc Farland
Lake Kegonsa
Cobb
Edmund
EL. 1221
Dodgeville
Mt. Vernon
L. Kegonsa
Utica
Linden
Jonesdale
Daleyville
Paoli
Oregon
Stoughton
Mineral Point
Mifflin
Hollandale
Basco
Belleville
Brooklyn
Rewey
Waldwick
New Glarus
Dayton
Kodatz
Blanchardville
Cooksville
FIRST CAPITOL STATE PARK
Leslie
Stewart
Evansville
Attica
Fulton
Belmont
Calamine
Fayette
Monticello
Magnolia
Truman
Darlington
Lamont
Elkgrove
Argyle
GREEN
Albany
Footville
Jordan
Stearns
Wood ford
Elmo
LAFAYETTE
Meekers
Wiota
Benton
Shullsburg
EL. 1020
Dill
Monroe
EL. 1035
Juda
Orfordville
Brodhead
Gratiot
Browntown
Dunbarton
New Diggings
CHARLES
S. Wayne
Clarno
Twin Grove
Newark
Avon
Martintown